The Immortal Sisterhood

The Immortal Sisterhood

12 Guiding Stars to Grow, Heal and Navigate Life

gemma cairney

CANONGATE

First published in Great Britain in 2026
by Canongate Books Ltd, 14 High Street, Edinburgh EH1 1TE

canongate.co.uk

1

British Library Cataloguing-in-Publication Data
A catalogue record for this book is available on
request from the British Library

ISBN 9781837267101

Typeset in Garamond by Biblichor Ltd, Scotland

Printed and bound by CPI Group (UK) Ltd, Croydon CR0 4YY

The manufacturer's authorised representative in the EU for
product safety is BGC Sustainability & Compliance,
7 avenue du Général Leclerc, Paris 75014
(gpsr@baldwinglobalconsulting.com)

MIX
Paper | Supporting
responsible forestry
FSC® C013604

This book is for Alpharita, for I see you and I always will.

You can't be what you can't see.

Marian Wright Edelman

within these pages there is both lament and awe //
within these pages I explore the potential of literary ritual.

gemma cairney

CONTENTS

Author's Note xi

1. Wang Zhenyi 1
2. Pamela Colman Smith 17
3. Una Marson 43
4. Audre Lorde 65
5. Jeanne Duval 87
6. Grace Jones 109
7. Marsha P. Johnson 129
8. Mary Wollstonecraft 153
9. Nanny of the Maroons 169
10. Mary Seacole 181
11. Betty Davis 199
12. Pharaoh Hatshepsut 227

Afterword 243
Notes 255
Bibliography 263
Acknowledgements 265

AUTHOR'S NOTE

When I set out to write this book, it was going to be a simple collection of love letters to 12 great women – whose individual and collective lives have more than inspired me. I wanted to write about how each of their legacies has offered me personal comfort in times of despair, loss, confusion and the strain of operating within systems where I often feel misunderstood. I wanted to thank this group of survivors: those who'd survived the hurt of rejection, heartbreak and harm by still leaving their mark regardless.

The more I wrote and researched these women, the more I understood how much I owed to their style of life, to the way they expressed themselves, to what they did with their time and creativity. And the more I researched, the more it became clear to me that I am in a world where the stories of those women whose shoulders I stand on can be so readily appropriated / fetishised and forgotten.

I realised I was going to need to go beyond the letters I'd originally planned. I stepped into the wilds: I started noticing all the patterns, the fractals, the mycelial connections to our womanhood and humanity. Roots of information about one of the Sisters would lead to poignant revelations about another. The Sisters appeared in my dreams. Beat poetry came through my fingertips and between my hips as I learned about the mistreatment many of the Sisters experienced and saw the similarities to some of my own troubling times and those of other **womxn** I know. These stories, my stories, our stories, felt vividly interconnected. As I developed *The Immortal Sisterhood* as a concept, the chapters of my own life continued to unfold in harmony with the chapters and the Sisters within them – despite echoes of tumult.

While writing this book, I went from art lover to artist, moved country from England to Scotland, noticed the neurodivergence within myself, started to read tarot, entered my forties, and, most monumentally, became a mother – a role that wrapped around the many others I breathe within.

My thirties had been thrilling. Newly single, high-earning, giddy, a homeowner, a bit artsy, even a bit famous! My mind had often been lost in formative eras of British nostalgia for punk-spirited Cool Britannia – a hall of mirrors made up of distorted pub mindlessness / booziness, rave culture, opulence, nightlife and shopping under a male gaze.

Then, all of a sudden, an inescapable yet enticing riptide of social media emerged, offering quick-hit validation. Content and time were now being experienced through headphones, consumed alone on screens streaming individualised 'anything', from porn to action films at any moment.

It was all scrutiny and face fillers and blue-lit dopamine. We all felt this change in our bodies. Digital dependency became vital to ordinary life. If you were ambitious, or even in the public eye, the chasm between creating opportunity in the real world versus a virtual one got so big it was hard for us all to keep up – creators and consumers alike. I don't think many of us knew how much all this access to, well, everything, could be as horrifying as it could be positive, or how much it would start dictating and constraining everyone's psyche and behaviour in the urge to comply with it all.

Unexpectedly, around my mid-thirties, language about mental health in general exploded. Our inner worlds, past traumas and all the weaving of lived experience wrapped up in Western culture began to be unearthed to dizzying effect. It felt very different from the trance of my twenties. From the age of 23, I'd been working in fields of creativity: live on radio, hosting events (often to a corporate brief), meeting pop stars for money. But I found that even with a loud voice, a non-stop inquisitive nature and a love of people, I was increasingly having to shout louder and contort myself to behave in response to cookie-cutter algorithms. It became about trends instead of tribes. About a hunger for what could be served up quickly / kept young, replacing the slow-cooked maturing of curation / public figures and ideas.

My body – in contrast to the shiny material things I'd been able to obtain – wanted something different. I started having nightmares. I lived at the sea's edge in Margate on the southeast coast of England, where the promise of voyage confronted me daily and sirens beckoned me to travel. I woke up one night gasping. Why couldn't I breathe? Night terrors. Shame. // Memories. // Fragmentation. // Grief. How was there so much fear in my body? I was busy. I'd grown up poor and suddenly I wasn't anymore, and it was because of a job that was all about 'personality' – so I had to keep mine HAPPY, or I would be poor again.

How could I steady myself when everything in my feeds was feeding so fast and felt numbing? If it was possible for me to be thinking the scariest thing in the middle of the night and playing it out in my dreams, maybe it was possible to save myself too. I knew I wasn't the only one. So many of us have lived through trauma and commotion, even losing trust in the mere act of living. I wasn't yearning for happiness. I was yearning for hope. The sorrow I felt about growing up and realising it was a lie that security and worth could be found in the material wasn't just my experience. It was part of a bigger, interlinked web of inherited memories, a haunting of late-stage capitalism and the slow untethering of global trust connected to all women everywhere.

I started to read more widely. I started to look up. It led me north, to Scotland, to its landscape of sublimity, from where my mother-line stems. My mind / body began growing like a tree, stronger, deeply rooted. I became more connected to humanity, to magic. The process of writing about other lives – the Sisters – worked in unison as I faced a reckoning about my own life. I lost and found myself many times during the process of writing this book. I reckoned with great female friends dying: one (an outstanding artist) from cervical cancer; the other (the most charismatic TV presenter I've ever met) by suicide. I mourned and escaped in time travel by immersing myself in the creativity and style of the activist Marsha P. Johnson, who innovated with transgressive fashion by reusing everyday items, and embodied deep care and activism in New York in the 1970s. I could see these same acts of invention in the medicinal techniques of the nineteenth-century Jamaican nurse and businesswoman Mary Seacole before her, who had a knack for applying healing poultices to the bodies of the wounded. I felt uplifted by realising how often I've found myself in the places once occupied by these incredible women. Even if history had tried to erase them, the Sisterhood had always been there. I just hadn't found them yet. I was part of them now and they a part of me, patterning me.

Moving home from the chalky cliffs of the English Channel in Margate to the marl and dense sandstone of Edinburgh, I started learning more about the intricate skills and crafts of women in history who were deemed witches worthy of murder. When mostly they were actually midwives, medicine women, healers, apothecaries and artists / but the public murders of many of these women took place within walking distance of where I now sleep / witch hunts normalised by historical fact. Driven by patriarchal fear / of how magical we are. I now know how our magic is everywhere: in our words, our art, our medicine, our cycles, our mothering (whether we have children or not) / all keeping us as connected to Earth's core and allowing us to soar high enough to even create rainbows should we wish.

I love women and our potential.

The late African American playwright, poet, author and activist, Ntozake Shange, used her pen like a machete. She devised a new art form that she called 'Choreopoetry' (blending drama / poetry / dance) and unapologetically used slashes // in many of her works, freeing the reader (or the audience of her live shows) from the potential oppression bound in the English language by creating a remixing of disciplines and quilting them together to make something new. I feel huge gratitude for Ntozake's boldness and have been inspired to use the same slash method throughout this book.

You can read this book any way you like: perform it, read it out loud, frenetically dance it. There are no rules.

Dance,
        shake,
ROAR
        through it whenever you need.

There's no judgement here.

It's all communication (a word originally rooted in care, from the word commūnicāre meaning to share in community).

This is a book written about sisterhoods – mine and yours:

our **hair roots**,
our **patterns**,
our **heartlands**,

our **bloodlines, motherlands, interconnections**,
our **purpose** and our **past lives.**

By learning about the way each of the women in *The Immortal Sisterhood* overcame adversity and how they moved through, loved and lived in a world where the odds were always against them, I have been offered inspiration for new ways of living in the now.

The poetry of The Immortal Sisterhood's lives has nurtured me in my present, and I would invite you to be open to the same. You'll notice there are different styles of poetry, memoir vignettes (which I call 'sense memories'), biography, supernaturalist visions, lore, imaginings and more in this book. I noticed that when I started to focus on the fullness of one of the Sisters and their story, and to work out how I wanted to revere them through this project, I was often no longer distracted by the tragedy they may have experienced. Something profound was able to happen in these pages. The human side of history became more important than scholarly pursuit, and I felt able to offer celebration to the sides of women that made them soothsayers, bards, troubadours, and wisdom-givers.

> The objective was to question the process of memorialisation that might silence or appropriate her instead of providing her with a safe space of memory.
>
> Mireille Rosello, essay on Jeanne Duval (see p.87)

As I researched the Sisters, I traced my own heritage and reframed physical travel as ritual and ceremony. I wrote all over the world. I studied astral processes and giggled with my childhood self, who had once had an open fascination with travelling through time. Suddenly, there they were, my 12, my Immortal Sisterhood, like stars that keep us pilgrims on track.

In this book, I present them all to you as an Immortal Sisterhood, each with something slightly different to offer; each with something connected to a part of me that, in admiration for them, I found a way to honour. Thanks to them, I found a way to accept and celebrate the parts of myself that I might have once thought damaged.

A lot of these women risked being written out of existence by history. As I immersed myself in the lives and work of each of them, I felt a new sense of agency surge through me. I felt it when I came across the music, life and mixed heritage of psychedelic style icon and funk musician Betty Davis, who is still mostly – maddeningly – only known as the 'wildest' of jazz musician Miles Davis's wives. Or when I learned about illustrator Pamela Colman Smith, who in 1909 designed and hand-drew the world's most commonly used set of tarot cards, and yet whose name appears nowhere on the pack.

These women – and their imaginary fellowship – have changed me. These pages are an ode to what they have to teach us all about survival and the choosing of a life full of brave wonder.

The Immortal Sisterhood

Introducing the Immortal Sisterhood – our constellation (ordered roughly by star sign where birthdates are known):

Wang Zhenyi – Born in 1768, China. A mathematical genius of expansive multi-talents who found codes from the moon and campaigned for education for all.

Pamela Colman Smith (aka 'Pixie') – Born in 1878, England. Painter, designer, occultist and shapeshifter, who was inspired by William Blake and went on to inspire William Butler Yeats through her charm, performance and visual art.

Una Marson – Born in 1905, Jamaica. Traveller, campaigner, broadcaster, and the first Black female voice broadcast on the BBC.

Audre Lorde – Born in 1934, USA. Poet, philosopher, professor, activist. She unapologetically championed Blackness and queerness, and wrapped it in poetry as a form of resistance.

Jeanne Duval – Born c.1820, likely Haiti. A sex-working sorcerer whose lure and presence made her the inspiration for the poetry of Charles Baudelaire in nineteenth-century Paris.

Grace Jones – Born in 1948, Jamaica. Musician, actress, and a force of nature who fused reggae, pop and disco. An icon for innovators and freedom seekers.

Marsha P. Johnson – Born in 1945, USA. A butterfly of style and expression, known as 'the mayor of Christopher Street' for her LGBTQ rights activism and involvement in the Stonewall riots, who understood the radical power and salvation of friendship for the most vulnerable.

Mary Wollstonecraft – Born in 1759, England. A pioneer, explorer, lover and women's rights activist, who showed women that we can and should move around this earth freely, regardless of our situation.

Nanny of the Maroons – Born c.1686, West Africa. A leader of the rebellion for the emancipation of enslaved people in Jamaica, who used ancient wisdom and tribal West African practice to heal and strategise.

Mary Seacole – Born in 1805, Jamaica. A healer, doctor, and herbalist, who campaigned for democratising access to health care in the Global North.

Pharaoh Hatshepsut – Born in 1507 BCE, Ancient Egypt. Gender-defying leader who excelled in architectural advancement, travel and trade, and overcoming trauma.

Betty Davis – Born in 1944, USA. Genre-bending singer, songwriter and troubadour who channelled musicality, rage and exertion through performance and lyricism.

A Glossary of Sorts

Chapter Threads

Each chapter carries its own small glossary – a set of threads woven through that Sister's story that you might want to pull on. They appear here in the order you'll have met them on the page, not alphabetically, because this book moves the way memory and discovery move: forward, associatively, one thing leading to another. Some threads are people, some are places, some are concepts or objects, and some are words that have been borrowed, reclaimed or totally, intuitively invented.

Sense Memory

In acting, the technique of 'sense memory' is taught to deepen an actor's understanding of the character they are embodying. The theory is that a certain sense may trigger a certain characteristic or memory of a person, affecting them both internally and externally. In *The Immortal Sisterhood*, I have borrowed the term for when I'm triggered or inspired by another Sister's experiences, regardless of how long ago they lived.

Sistxr Spellings

I use this 'x' frequently. It expresses an expansive and inclusive sistxrhood, immortalised beyond hatred and fear.

Sister Synchronicity

The sacred and embodied geometry connecting all of us. There is as much of the unexplained – of all the under-researched things we call 'woo woo' – as there isn't in these pages. Don't worry – you'll get used to it.

Snake Beat

In many traditions the snake's shedding of skin represents transformation and letting go. You'll notice a beat poem threaded through the text. It was written one day out of rage and a need to process the existence of subjugation throughout history.

Snake Beat PT I

Di-vest
Don't be afraid
to des-cribe
Deviate
Divergence
Emergence
Never Too Much
Never Too Late

Is it possible to live outside category?

p
        o
l
y
        m
        a

        t
        h
?

Dare women call themselves such? Dare we deviate from the colonial categories of Western understanding?

Can

I

be

a

witch

please?

Sister Synchronicity: Scary Spice, the early 1990s, somewhere in the home counties

Despite the fact I found glory in reading poetry and asking questions, I was regularly told I was 'bad at school'. The questions from my big mouth were deemed too frequent, and the sense that I was doing something wrong was cemented by the number of times I was told off by every kind of authority in all aspects of my life. I was punished with more detentions than most of my classmates, and was often called in for 'special tellings-off'. This treatment – as it often does – all added to a self-fulfilling prophecy that I see happen to lots of Black and brown young people growing up in places where our colouring can make us inferior to the prevailing whiteness that can dominate the representation around us. The kind of fury thrown at the 'unruly' child is targeted when you're of my complexion; the language used is specific / sometimes permeated with disgust / I was told my hair was 'uncontrollable', that my voice was 'far too loud', and that unless I learned how to suppress my curiosity and energy, I would amount to nothing.

I'm an adult now. Today, I feel clearer about all that . . . how it happened . . . how none of the mistreatment was my fault or deserved, and I have learned with all my body and my heart that I can rise into sunshine from the shadow // I'm no longer afraid of being 'too much'.

But this is the privilege of gentler reflection. I had no idea then, because I was just a child and doing all the living and working out for the first time, without much encouragement to be proud of myself / for who I might be and become.

My official school diaries from that time give me an actual physical experience when I hold them and turn the many curled pages marked with 'W's, meaning 'Warning'. The rule was that you would get three warnings and then that was it, you were 'on detention' – forced to sit alone and 'think about what you'd done'. It made for a tough and confusing experience. The contemplation time / the lambasting that ensued fed into years of masking need / I was repeatedly told I was bad. It was a hard feeling to escape when it was constantly reinforced at home and by the popular culture around me. The TV told me that the only Spice Girl who looked like me was the 'scary' one and that in the US – in a culture Britain looked up to and mimicked – the glamour and levels of fame available to you if you were Black were way, way higher if you allowed yourself to be hypersexualised.

As a child, I would imagine incessantly. I had a mind that constantly soared – without social media / influencers / non-stop information to lead me or distract me – as I tried to work everything out.

Why did I feel things so deeply?

Why were there so many tears in my house?

Why were adult relationships so complex in real life compared to films?

Why was my body the way it was?
Why did I have no sense of being in my own skin?

Why were my little sister and I the only ones with what we identified back then as brown skin after we moved to a town outside London?

I would scour books and magazines for hours to find understanding and to see my own face or experience represented somewhere. Time swirled differently: there were no mobile phones or laptops. I spent time creating my own stories of adventure, some about my favourite teddy bear – Prickles – travelling the world. I wrote poems that turned people into all colours of the rainbow, and kept a private diary which, when I read it back now, frighteningly oscillates between the expected innocence of a 10-year-old and a profound need for acceptance that feels beyond my years. There are self-portraits of me crying, with speech bubbles calling myself ugly in comparison to my friends. But the majority of the time, my imagination was a salvation. It was safety away from cultural, verbal and occasionally physical violence. None of that could take away the sparkling ambition // dreams of writing books, of creating theatre, of bringing communities together despite differences. Harm made this want for creativity surge in me even more. I knew that if we all came together we could inevitably find healing joy somehow, some way . . . Because laughing and smiling and dancing felt so much easier for our spirits than all the pain and all the strictness I would so often come across.

I was a child choreographing, scrapbooking and orchestrating her way out of adversity. All of those luminous habits would remain, of course. Singing in the garden. Echoing the moves of The Spice Girls, dressed as 'Scary', and Eternal (remember them?) because they offered an identifiable aesthetic, an attainable realness. I remember physically collaging booklets of all my dreams and stories, which I would design with colouring pens and cut-out photographs. I stapled the pages meticulously and protected them in sticky-back plastic, as though I was publishing my own work. The finessing and embellishing gave me indescribable satisfaction. I was healing myself again and again with my own imagination.

The now, somewhere in Scotland

Now I'm grown, with pride pumping in my heart, I can look back and know that I got through school and that, university or not, 'amounting to nothing' wasn't the case at all – I built a creative career, brick by brick. I worry, though, how creative subjects are viewed with such disregard in the school system. I hope that one day the fireworks of poetic and philosophical enrichment can become the norm for all of us in our everyday lives from the earliest age.

I can see now that my body and mind were searching for magic. But any sense of seeing things through a cross-cultural lens back then was totally non-existent, and for a long time, that created a void where my belonging should have been. For example, the only Black history I learned at school was about the traumatising horrors of the transatlantic slave trade, rather than on the organisation for emancipation among my ancestors. It's only through travel and introspection and live storytelling and reading certain progressive literature that I've found my true identity and unearthed gifts that could not have been found in the set of grades I received for my GCSEs. My potential certainly wasn't found in the 'W's' spelling out 'Warnings' inscribed in shame beside my name.

Inter-disciplines, **pedagogy** and diaspora are all things I have embraced later in life and I've been treated as though expressing myself in different forms is an indulgence, yet daily I see white, male counterparts permitted – encouraged, even – to explore their different skillsets, and deemed polymaths or cutting-edge masters and geniuses. The reality, though, is that there are so many women from the past and present who have worked and continue to work tirelessly at the vanguard of science and art and all the connective tissue in between – esotericism / nature / healing – who are scrutinised first and foremost for their life choices and not for the professional work they're doing to progress all of our lives. There are many polymaths // slashies // women and non-binary geniuses whose work should be revered but hasn't been.

By the time we're out in the working world, we're put into such easily segregated categories. But that's not how I – and many others – experience life. I'm a writer, producer, broadcaster, artist, mother, a slashie[1] and many other things besides.

Thankfully, in my Immortal Sisterhood, there is one Sister who showed me that embracing different talents and exploring varying forms of expression and skill is not only possible but was being done centuries before any of us were born.

Wang Zhenyi is our staunch polymath mind, with gifts so vast she was a walking contradiction of the idea that we can be either a words or a numbers person.

Chapter Threads

womxn – all women.

pedagogy – the method of practice or teaching.

1

Wang Zhenyi

The intersectional mathematician

'My mental wandering is inexhaustible.'

Wang Zhenyi

王貞儀 Wang Zhenyi
Born: 1768
Died: 1797
Sign: Unknown
Pronouns: She / Her

Born over 250 years ago, Zhenyi was an astronomer, a mathematician, a sorcerer of **STEM** and a prolific published poet. This sister gave us a literal understanding of the heavens and all in a short time on earth . . . Or 'ScienceMoon Spice' if you like . . .

Born in the Jiangsu province in southeast China in the early Qing dynasty to a family of intellectuals and scholars, Zhenyi was also a mastermind, and it showed from an early age. The elders in Wang's life provided a solid influence but it seems she knew books would act as allies, too. Her grandfather was known to have over 75 bookshelves and as a child she read through her grandfather's extensive book collection with intense curiosity. Not just works of literature and poetry, but also volumes of texts on numbers, the planets and the sky . . . all growing the seeds of potential within her to amalgamate her own concepts of multi-culture, democracy, science, equality and nature into the kaleidoscope that became her legacy.

She was just 14 when her grandfather died, and it would be another five years before she and her father left the region. She travelled extensively (something else that would open her mind). She used all of this formative time productively, reading ferociously from those 75 shelves, ploughing her way through books spanning subjects from arithmetic to biology.

Wang never went to school, though what she lacked in formal education she made up for with incessant home study, and in the encouragement she received from the different generations of her family and their friends. Her grandmother read with her and recommended different volumes of ancient Chinese folklore and poetry, while her Father taught her geography, mathematics and medicine. They were a family that enticed her to keep learning and not feel bound by categories, genres or fields.

A Sense Memory: Blossom

The 1990s & for ever

When I was just three, I leaped towards a woman in our local playground. 'Hello, my name's Gemma,' I beamed. 'I'm going to be famous one day,' I told her, very sure, but of course without knowing how corrosive I'd one day find fame to be. This woman was beautiful, and she had a little girl the same size as my baby sister at the time. I'd made a beeline for her, my arms outstretched in innocence. Blossom ended up becoming a family friend for life and, though I was never officially given godparents, from that day I have always had this woman I bounded over to in my life. She and my mum started talking that day and it turned out we all lived very close and their kids were similar in age: two amazing women both with mixed-race daughters and lives of many moving parts, both soul-filled, life-loving women in the early nineties, excited by all that was being laid out for them. My mum worked in marketing and could speak French. Blossom was a mature student in her late twenties studying a Black history and Western Philosophy degree and practised yoga. Both these women, at this time, were living embodiments of motherHOOD and its many parts and contradictions, including the fact that this guiding force of 'The HOOD' when it comes to all things – MOTHER – can be extended to everything we care about and want to protect: how to carve out an illustrious life as an example to others, how to evolve your career, how to develop a deeper understanding of nature and a respect for the importance of community and kin, and how to hold and pass on the stories within us all – of our mothers and their mothers, and their friends and confidantes. All can be Mother.

This deeper sense of hood in the practice of mothering goes way beyond giving birth to a baby. It's in the mother that is earth and the multiple mothers we love and the nurture we pour into everything living.

Blossom has continued to provide joy and counsel my whole life – whether that was asking me to be a bridesmaid at her wedding when I was seven and me ecstatically choosing sparkly shoes for the occasion, or many years later, being on the other end of the phone in the middle of the night, listening to me when I was very low and afraid. Many women have shown me a love more motherly than I could have known had I expected it all from just one human.

There is Mother in plants, the types of plants that might sting but can survive harsh conditions and contain healing properties when treated right, like nettles. There is Mother in flowers that burst through our subconscious with beauty, the animals that we are drawn to in awe and our keepsakes such as gold rings that get passed down families for generations.

Wang was known to take long trips from her teens, each extending the sense of wanderlust she felt throughout her life and that pulses through her every written word. The impact of the landscape she experienced is clear in many of her writings too. By the time she was in her early twenties she was writing poetry about her trips.

> So important is the doorway,
> occupying the throat of the mountain
> Looking down from the heaven,
> The sun sees Yellow river streaming.
>
> Wang Zhenyi, 'Transiting Tong Pass'

This is an extract of a poem written about one of her many expeditions. It's little surprise that her poetry is influenced by her travels and vice versa. She captures the power and raw beauty of travelling through nature with an aliveness that reminds me that much of this world has been so naturally astonishing for so long. It also acts as a reminder to me as a soul seeker and researcher that nature writing at its best is like reading spells of preservation – it's timeless and speaks to a collective soul that yearns to save the planet from the destruction of climate change today.

Wang took long trips across China not just for the sake of leisure but to cultivate experience and build knowledge. This makes me want to study themes of exploration and its documentation by womxn.

Ever since reading the translated excerpt of 'Transiting Tong Pass' by Sister Wang, I've been thinking about the actual sound the throat of the mountain might make . . . I'm taken back to the throat singing I experienced while working in the country of Georgia, to make an episode of *The Sound Odyssey*[1] with Welsh Sister – **Charlotte Church**. We were there to capture a collaboration between Charlotte and a choir made up of male **polyphonic** singers. The sound was melancholy, very, very old, and a form of guttural expression I had never heard of before this assignment. Would the throat of the mountain sound the same? Haunting, beckoning and inviting us to bellow out a grief stored deep in our bellies? Is that how the mountain sounds?

Just as few women explorers and travellers from history are known or celebrated today, so, too, are women of science and mathematics frequently sidelined. Zhenyi, remarkably, excelled in all these interests in her single life. There's always been an implicit need for women to channel their experience and values into world-changing knowledge. Not only are odysseys, expeditions, adventures and pilgrimages worth taking from an individual perspective, but when the thinking and art they inspire are documented (for example, through poetry, paintings, music, letters, documentaries) those works then stand as eternal pillars to support and sustain generations of explorers to come. Imagine Wang Zhenyi, Charlotte Church, **Nan Shepherd**, **Isobel Wylie Hutchinson**, **Puka Puka** and **Kuiyecoke** next to one another at a dinner party. What stories of wisdom and travel would they exchange?

What would connect them? A passion for land? A familiar deep sense of justice? A respect for female friendship? Would Wang talk about her love of horse riding?

She had a love of riding, archery and martial arts – apparently born from spending time with the wife of a local Mongolian

Army General. The Qing government / dynasty of China during Zhenyi's lifetime defined itself as a 'multi-ethnic' state, which included surrounding territories such as Mongolia and Tibet. Cultural influence would have been far from homogenised. Wang understandably found nationalism limiting:

> What counts is the usefulness, no matter whether it is Chinese or Western.
>
> Wang Zhenyi[2]

The more I learn about our polymath's unique story, the more I'm compelled and astounded by her. She lived in an age long before education for women became the norm. How did she tackle such wide-ranging, complex subjects without the confidence that formal academia gives a person? Was she perhaps a testament to the idea that filling a life with things you love brings you a general grounding and pride that can feed into everything you do? Is having pastimes that fill your cup enough to give you energy to flourish in your career?

In China, where Wang roamed and excelled, a secret language was at its height in the Hunan district. It was called Nüshu and was spoken by women-only groups, who shared an invented language meant for one another only. It was often coded in embroidered cloth and designed as an act of care to uplift and offer unconditional support for whatever the women were experiencing. These acted as webs of shared and expressed hopes, dreams, griefs and passions, woven without the glare of patriarchal interference. I long for secret symbols for the now: womxn to womxn symbols that cannot be judged by anyone except the trusted tribe, each symbol or word having a meaning that creates resonance to protect us on a huge scale, but with such silence and stealth that the power it gives would make it impossible to dominate us.

Wang, meanwhile, was making her own one-woman counter culture. Over the course of her life, she published at least 12 works. Her work disproved the notion that women used 'flowery language'. She often wrote in the Ci style, a classical form traditionally known for its lyrical style, which can be set to music.

In the artistic form, coined by **Laurie Anderson**, called Music Theatre today, repetitive movement is performed with experimental scores of music. It has me wondering how Wang's Ci poetry could be read with music.

Wang would go on to take her mathematical genius and fuse it into her work with equal rights. She believed education should be democratised, and published simplified understandings of numbers and calculation so they could be accessible to all. *The Simple Principles of Calculation*, her best-known work, was published when she was 24 years old. By simplifying mathematics, Zhenyi was a radical of her time. Trigonometry, time theory and astronomy were all subjects gate-kept by men of wealth and power. Wang became a master of them all.

Knowledge has always been ring-fenced by the elite. But when those in positions of privilege rethink how knowledge can be made accessible, it unlocks equality for everyone. Wang did exactly this. Money, finance and numbers are intertwined (lest we forget), and it was on her formative travels – as a woman from a well-off dynasty – that she came to viscerally notice the disparity of rich and poor. She unashamedly wrote about the injustice she saw around her:

> Village is empty of cooking smoke,
> Rich families let grains stored decay;
> In wormwood strewed pitiful starved bodies,
> Greedy officials yet push farm levying

Wang Zhenyi, 'Poem of eight lines' (Extract)

She always had her eyes open and processed what she saw through poetry. She leveraged her bravery and huge privilege to write books and teach others. She didn't just have enormous competence. She was *driven*. She was a woman who realised what she saw and then put the effort into the 'doing' of making things change. The threshold between thought and documentation / idea and physical experiment / a desire to learn and stewarding the lessons for others (a process I find fascinating): time after time, she took the leap to do what she saw as right.

Sister Synchronicity: Feminist activations

> Are you not convinced,
> Daughters can also be heroic?
>
> Wang Zhenyi[3]

I actually thought about Jane Austen while I was reading about Wang Zhenyi because in *Among Women*, a book about Jane Austen's private world and the women that she was with and the women that she spent time with, the way that they spoke to each other was totally different from the way they presented themselves outside of women's circles. It's almost like that intimate sharing of 'knowing' – or a physical space where you get your cautionary tales from – was integral for the women who broke through the limitations of the past. Is it our mum, our sister, a particular circle of friends? Or aunt? It made me think about where our resources and networks of information are? A secret subversion. The books then came from a library because of privilege and access . . . but now we have access to many, I'd invite us to ask ourselves who is the person or real-life ally who first told you

> that you were allowed to subvert the status quo? Who gives you the permission? When we look back at Feminist history it's so often a secret voice who encourages you, beyond education.
>
> Songwriter, musician and author Emma-Lee Moss when I spoke to her about what the life of Wang Zhenyi inspired her to think.

Wang didn't stop at trigonometry either. She took the heavens into her own hands when she noticed that the solar eclipse was yet to be really explained. She went about experimenting with a round table in an outdoor pavilion in her garden, using a hanging crystal lamp and a mirror to represent the Earth, Sun and the Moon's movements, and to make precise measurements to demonstrate the moon's phases. Wang's teachings on celestial phenomena, the planets and lunar and solar eclipses all feed into our scientific understandings of astronomy today.[4] She was even one of the first scientists to argue against the idea that the world was flat, in her paper 'Theory of the Roundness of Earth'. It was almost insanely bold of Wang to challenge what had long been seen in society as a supernatural phenomenon. During this period in China, the Qing Imperial Court employed people to accurately 'predict' eclipses, to signify the emperor's legitimacy through 'the mandate of heaven'. In Chinese mythology, pre-dating Wang's life by hundreds of years, it was told that a dragon or heaven dog – 天狗 (literally 'sun eat') – consumed the sun or moon during eclipses.[5] Wang, instead, explained them scientifically.

Before Wang's death, she gave instructions to her husband to deliver what was left of her manuscripts to her friend Madam Kuai. It turns out that at the end of her life it was a fellow woman Wang Zhenyi trusted the most to safeguard her works.

Scholarly study and a global outlook was a way of life for Wang. In the province where she grew up, there are now more than 16 universities there and more institutions of higher education than anywhere else in China. I like to think that it was her influence – even if just in spirit – that made this possible. Even so, today, womxn are still significantly underrepresented in STEM fields globally.

Zhenyi shows how both enjoyment and investigation can be part of our intellectual potential as women: a reciprocity can occur between love and work. Wang Zhenyi's legacy is one of opposites and of things she 'shouldn't' have been able to do. And it's proof that when we ignore these barriers, we can make even world breakthroughs happen.

L

i

m

i

t

s

are

conditioned.

March 2022

In the middle of the sea between the
North of England and the Netherlands

Dear Wang

I'm writing this from a small solo cabin on an overnight crossing from Newcastle in the North of England to a port in Amsterdam in the Netherlands. They say AI, algorithms and screens are changing the shape of our minds. My generation has been drowned in a homogeneous multiverse run by tech billionaires. Books are written about it, research is undertaken about it, formal discussion is had on it all – the W's of 'Warnings' are all in capitals, and though we mortals know through these alarm bells and our strained necks that it doesn't quite feel right, we can't seem to stop using it all. The most popular phones in the world right now are iPhones and the information that the cobalt inside them is mined by people (often children) in the Democratic Republic of the Congo – which faces genocide and civil war and is beholden to the biggest corporations in the world – is readily available. But we can't seem to stop.

In protest, I'm smartphone-free at the moment and I'm finding that, in general, I keep looking up, towards the tops of buildings, staring at the sky, looking for patterns in bird flocks. I have solitary and silent ceremony when I drink in a sunset. I say solitary because everyone around me is usually looking at their phones. So was I until I decided to try out this experiment with a **burner** for as long as I can. I was inspired by a trip I took to Addis Ababa, Ethiopia in 2019 where I was working on a radio documentary about Ethio-Jazz and found myself on an afternoon off, doing my favourite thing, wandering, and noticed that so many folk were buzzing about in the streets but not on mobiles, and it made for an atmosphere of smiles and busy harmony. Many say they 'couldn't live without their phones', as so much of our lives is now bound to a device: transaction, interaction, automation, organisation. But I'm enjoying finding ways out of the labyrinth, especially on this journey, navigating my way from Edinburgh to Stockholm.

In this act of 'just being' since functioning with just a simple burner, I am looking up, my body is reminded of how slow and gentle and silly we all are. I've been able to engage with the intuitive quality of friendships and I find that if I'm lacking the voice of certain friends, I call them on my **housephone** that I've installed, where the quality of sound and the feeling of the handset bring a different and tactile energy. I'm giving myself so much more time to meet people, as I don't have a quick 'running late' WhatsApp message as an option anymore.

I am liberated. Immersed into what Sister Audre (see Chapter 4) would describe as 'the erotic', in her essay 'Uses of the Erotic' published in 1978, she asks us this:

> Of course women so empowered are dangerous. So we are taught to separate the erotic demand from the most vital areas of our lives other than sex. And the lack of concern for the erotic root and satisfactions of our work

> is felt in our disaffection from so much of what we do. For instance, how often do we truly love our work even at its most difficult?

I would debate, that such disempowering capitalism has become so under questioned in our everyday lives that those of us who identify as women are doing so much more work than we ever have, and that it makes it even more difficult to 'truly' love and find pleasure or satisfaction in everything we do. But here I am, not bound to a device, and the freedom to forge my own dreams in the day is only accentuating my capacity for the erotic. Both selfhood and connection are available to me in a way they weren't before, balanced in **Yin & Yang**. I've made a pact to look into the eyes of fellow travellers, towards the stars rather than at a screen . . . I didn't even know this boat from Newcastle to Amsterdam existed until I gave myself this challenge of travelling plane-free. I'm noticing time expanding without a smartphone. Real life, maps and all their possibilities are appealing to the explorer inside me. I've made committed plans with fresh ink and my hands are clasping a paper itinerary, stapled together with the same intentional excitement and care I had when I assembled scrapbooks as a child. I never knew this could be so profound. I've felt natural sleep rhythms returning. I've cleared mind–space to notice the serendipity and riddles that stretch out before us almost every minute. The sea outside the window of my cabin swirls in the shape of a shell around a lighthouse and I've not seen anything so epic and beautiful for a long time.

What gave you the idea to study the moon's phases? Did you see any shooting stars as you stared skywards? Were you ever tempted to dance naked and alone in the garden in the dead of night?

Did you feel that all things are interconnected? Even things that are deemed as entirely opposite? Were mathematical calculations going through your head when you wrote poetry? Did you see routes out of socioeconomic disparity when you travelled, after witnessing both dynasty and poverty?
Thank you for the contrasts you fused together. Thank you for your determination. What you did lights a match on subverting what might be expected of us womxn all these years later.

Cultural braids

In Chinese culture, spiral patterns depict the interconnectedness of the universe and the everlasting interplay between opposing forces. In Celtic symbolism, the single swirl / spiral represents expansion, growth, the sun and birth. Though it dates back even further, it can be found marked on prehistoric sites, for example, in the motifs found on rock at Newgrange in County Meath, Ireland, which date back to 3200 BCE.

Chapter Threads

STEM – acronym for Science, Technology, Engineering and Mathematics.

Charlotte Church – a famous Welsh singer-songwriter born in 1986 who had her first No.1 single when she was 12 years old.

polyphonic – sound involving many voices where two or more parts have a melody of their own.

Nan Shepherd – Scottish walker, poet and writer (published by my publisher) born in 1893.

Isobel Wylie Hutchison – Scottish traveller, botanist and film-maker born in 1889.

Puka Puka and Kuiyecoke – the first women at the start of time in the lore of the Batammaliba people of Northern Togo and Benin.

Laurie Anderson – renowned North American avant-garde artist, filmmaker and performance artist born in 1947.

burner – a basic mobile phone with limited features, often prepaid, used as an alternative to smartphones.

housephone – a device installed in most homes, once upon a time connected by magic to wires across lands and sea so that we people can speak to each other.

Yin & Yang – a Chinese philosophy for opposites in balance, Yin representing dark, the feminine, rest, stillness and Yang representing light, the masculine and brightness.

2

Pamela Colman Smith

Painter, designer, occultist and shapeshifter

'Banish fear, brace your courage, place your ideal high up with the sun.'

Pamela Colman Smith, 'Should The Art Student Think', *The Craftsman*, 1908[1]

Born: 16 February 1878, Pimlico, London, United Kingdom
Died: 18 September 1951, Bude, United Kingdom
Sign: Aquarius
Pronouns: She / Her

Now we travel to the early 1900s where the self-proclaimed 'goddaughter of a witch' and 'sister to a fairy' ricocheted transatlantically and created a remarkable yet forgotten legacy.

Pamela
Colman
Smith
is a woman I adore to time-travel for.

'Strange little creature' are the words her peer **Arthur Ransome** uses to describe her in his 1907 book ***Bohemia in London***, and as I dive deeper into the life of Pamela, it's amazing how often language with 'strange' / 'creature-like' connotations comes up around her name. She was at the centre of the most cutting-edge interdisciplinary art scene of the time. You would have thought those people would have been completely open to the weird and the wonderful 'Pixie', as she was known. And yet . . . Here's my secret belief: lurking underneath this long-running habit of creaturifying / othering women like Pamela Colman Smith is nothing but . . . envy. Which of the male artists around her wouldn't have wanted to be as boldly talented and disarmingly eccentric as Pixie was?

Pamela was born in Pimlico, London, in 1878. Her parents had married in New York, where they'd both grown up. 'Melia' was the nickname given to her in honour of her maternal grandmother, Pamelia Chandler Colman, a prolific children's author. But it was an alternative nickname that ended up sticking throughout her life and that was 'Pixie' – an appropriately catchy and whimsical identity that offers us hints to the untameable **fae** energy of this Sister.

Uniqueness was in her blood. Her mother's side was full of artists, writers and booksellers, many of whom were practising Swedenborgians, (a smaller and more leftfield denomination of the Christian Church that focuses on inner spiritual growth, acts of service, and non-judgemental inclusivity). Her father's side was dominated by prominent industrialists and influential Puritan clergy folk, some of whom were even behind the growth of New York from a village to a city in the early nineteenth century.

At the age of 10 she moved with her family from London to Kingston, Jamaica, for her father's work on the railways. It was here that she was captivated by Jamaican folk tales and learned about the famed spider with a human head, Anansi: a mythological character who appears in old West African stories and along the **aural-heart-lines** that run across the seas to the Caribbean, acting as a wisdom-keeper and clever trickster who teaches us that knowledge shouldn't be hidden away by gatekeepers.

By the time Pixie was 15 she had relocated to New York City, before heading to London and back to Jamaica, creating an intensely diverse pot of references in her formative years. In the bustle of NYC in the mid-1890s she enrolled at the esteemed Pratt Institute to study composition, drawing and painting. She never graduated, beginning a theme that comes up again and again in her life, of always being on the move, always reinventing and starting again. She may have been creatively nomadic, but there's a vigour and persistence to the projects she undertook. And she did a lot of them.

Even though she did not graduate from the Pratt Institute, she was the first person to exhibit non-photographic work at the Alfred Stieglitz Photography Gallery in New York City in 1907, where she showed 72 of her watercolour artworks. Her style and persona puzzled people everywhere. She wore a hodgepodge of clothes from all over the world. Her dark hair and features made her difficult to place or label. She drew crowds in. But I think her exuberance pushed people away, too.

She spent many stints in London and Kent, prolifically mixing her interests in puppetry, visual arts, storytelling and vaudeville by relentlessly creating wherever she went. In her early works, Pixie demonstrated how much Jamaica had left a lasting effect on her as she meticulously created puppet shows depicting a genderless spider she called Annancy, beguiling curious audiences with her servings of 'Opal Hush' which was essentially a mixture of Claret and lemonade that created purple-gemstone-like bubbles. Writers would come to hang out for hours at her gatherings where magicians, dancers and folklorists all rubbed shoulders with each other.

Sister Synchronicity

London in the early to mid-2000s was still digitally lo-fi. The flash of club-photographers' bulbs caught the flailing for freedom on dance floors and sometimes (if you were lucky) would feature your brightly-lit image on a cool blog with a cult-following. It was the 'done thing' to cultivate an underground alter ego of dressing up and playing raucously and late into the night. There were different tribes and scenes that I bounced between in my tireless, extroverted, ingénuous early twenties . . . Sometimes I was blessed with making it to a Soho postcode where I could sip cheap vodka amid the gay community and the exquisitely styled club kids in a glorious scrum of ambiguity. My eyes delighted in the life and the dancing and the effort of the extraordinary and the laughter of London back then. Other times I would find myself lured into the dark of a lock-in in a room behind a mattress in the doorway of a pub on the Holloway Road called Nambucca. This was where I first discovered Florence Welch before her machine: a young witch with cascading flames for locks, tilting back on a piano with a wilding ability to spellbind us with song even then. It's there that I listened to the early haunting transcendent lyrics of a teenage Laura Marling and all the boys in bands wore sweat smelling leather that sparked pheromones as they played guitar or bass and told us stories in smoked-out voices like bards of yesteryear. I only cared about the moment, the organic, and the unexpected. I didn't scrutinise how recklessness might affect me then because I was swept up in the haze, the glow of music, fashion, art and hipness. It was a feral time for creativity in England's capital city back then, the more DIY the more exciting, the more undefinable and secret the more applauded. I remember once sitting in The Old Blue Last in the East End. The pub was owned by a magazine called

Vice, which was worth an awful lot of money and sweeping through youth culture back then. Little did I know that years later multiple allegations would erupt from this mag, with accusations of sexual harassment in the workplace. For those of us who didn't identify as men, there was this feeling that we were searching for ways to reach the stars, and art was portrayed as absolute desire (an escapist paradigm perhaps?) in which we could be protected from the everlasting imprint of misogyny.

Pixie's Quest

'Pigs! the publishers are all pigs!?!' Pamela writes of the publishing industry in 1901 in a letter to her friend, editor Albert Bigelow Paine. By which point, she had been exhausted by constantly pitching and constantly being underpaid.

Her earlier days of salon hosting had resulted in friendships with most of the who's-who in artsiness, folk, journalism and literature of the day between Ireland, England and the US's East Coast . . . This included **Bram Stoker**, **William Butler Yeats** and **Ellen Terry** . . . all figures written about and revered extensively since. Their work was praised for its complexities and radical ideas. Whereas Pamela Colman Smith is hardly ever heard of.

By 1914 the guest book for her weekly hosting of soirées had stopped. Pixie is said to have cited the reason as 'she didn't care for people anymore' and moved into her next phase, another first of many . . .

Quantum leaps; senses

Pamela is documented as having had a neurological condition called **synaesthesia,** a rarity that I've come across in some of the most artistic and enigmatic people I know. It's arguably a superpower: a perceptual phenomenon in which stimulation of one sensory or cognitive pathway leads to involuntary experiences in a second sensory or cognitive pathway. (Mary J. Blige has a type that turns sound into colour. Billie Eilish can visualise music with graphic detail and textural landscape.) In short, one sense is replaced with another. Smell for seeing colours, maybe, seeing colours for sound or hearing sonics and seeing shapes or visions. In the case of Pamela, she painted 'Music Pictures' from seeing visuals from very specific pieces of composition. For Beethoven's *Sonata No. 11* it was a giant, cloaked woman emerging from the mountains and looking down at a humble visitor.

> When I see equations, I see the letters in colours. I don't know why. I see vague pictures of Bessel functions with light-tan, j's, slightly violet-bluish, n's, and dark brown, x's flying around.
>
> Synaesthesia described by physicist Richard Feynman, who won the Nobel Prize for Physics in 1965 and whose work explained a clear and defining path to quantum physics.

Sense & Synchronicity

I've often thought that dancing is more important to me than so much in my everyday life. Not for any outcome except to stomp through unwanted emotion. I was sad when craft beer establishments took over all those dives with small lit-up dance floors when Friday and Saturday nights were about being 'in-our-cups' / drinking, talking over the beats and exulting in irony with drinking buddies over harmonising friendships in dance moves. The kinds of friendships where everything was on the table / the tables we danced upon.

There were colours I saw, hope in those notes / beats / rainbows.

Tai-Chi-effect 90s slow dances, in blues /

hip-shaking latinx-pop-reverence smooshed in orange.

Potential kisses, dancehall-mash-ups shimmering in green and gold.

In 1903 Pamela painted a watercolour called 'The Wave'. It depicts seven women, in wave-spirit form, curling abstractly into the tides. They are melded into one another by gradient shades of blue; one of them is crying drippy tears back into the water from which they've emerged. The sea is made up of their everlasting bodies. The sky they rise into is black. As I gaze at this picture, I am reminded of the essence of the combination of night and sea. It makes me wonder if we're closest to phases of grief at night: emotions otherwise submerged into our subconscious in the light of day? When there's too much to do, too much at stake to become water. There's the element of the sea, the element I'm connected to most . . . a vast mass of salt water that has helped me heal again and again, a real and metaphorical body of water that has tended to my aching limbs, washed away my tears and brought me right back into a romance with mysticism. Waves have quite literally birthed me into maturity and crashed away the blues of growing up. I know from experience that if I am lucky enough to be in the vicinity of the sea when feeling melancholy, then I am offered a chance to truly release – her mercy, her changes, her secrets and our trust can guide us into letting go of all that fucks with us.

Enticement, magick, movement, spirituality, artistic resistance, levity: it's all in the sea and I think Pamela knew this when she painted this picture. Did she hear it too?

Upcoming Sister Audre Lorde mentions the goddess **Yemanja**[2] and water in one of her poems:

I become myself an incantation
darn raucous characters
leaping back and forth across bland pages
Mother Yemanja raises her breasts to begin my labor
near water

– a line from 'The Winds Of Orisha' by Audre Lorde originally published in 1973 in her collection *From A Land Where Other People Live.*

'The Wave' reminds me of our collective emotion and infectious ability – the idea that we are in fact not alone in these moments – there is a place where we may have tears during witching hours.

When I cry into oceans
others do too

for interlinked reasons

Among the commotion of this noisy world, our ancestors converge with the stirring mermaids and hear us, above it all.

Pamela ended up joining the **Hermetic Order of The Golden Dawn***, a secret society that studied and merged the practice of Western esotericism, Egyptian magic, tarot and astrology, and was permeated by the Masonic structure common at the time. It was here she met the publisher / poet and mystic who would have a huge impact on her legacy: Arthur Edward Waite.

Her social life became more focused. She was invited to idyllic places and collaborated on projects in a variety of disciplines. On Ellen Terry's estate she drew and designed costumes for ballet shows. The fact that Pamela was never given the same prestige as her peers despite the vast range and body of her work speaks volumes. So much of her work is just as complex and multi-faceted and should be regarded as great, but her name got lost somehow. Why? Was it something to do with the fact that she appeared racially ambiguous? Too hard to pinpoint? Too hard to define her fusing of many forms? Too out-there and unruly, and therefore easier and simpler to erase?

Sister Synchronicity: Rejection

December 2025

My somatic response to rejection these days has me searching for practices and processes that help my body to learn that some of the no's / the non-starts / comparisons and the endings are just not as personal as they all seem. They're often just my refusal to stay within the realms of what's 'palatable'. When I know I'm safe and in the arms of the radical and the weird, I get to create resilience for the rejection those things will make me susceptible to. I dance, make spaghetti on many days of the week, write more, watch documentaries about the other weirdos who stuck it out. I was told 10 years ago that I was not 'girly enough' to be seen for a job I was completely qualified for. This feedback was so glib that my exasperation became laughter. What exactly *am* I 'enough' of?

The Tarot Deck

Many times in her life, Pamela exited the scene or cohort she'd been in. Before she left the Hermetic Order of The Golden Dawn, she created 78 designs for a new tarot deck, commissioned by Arthur Edward Waite.

Tarot had been practised in different ways for many years in the West, having originated from ancient **Kemet**, where the Book of Thoth was studied and praised as wisdom from the god of writing and magic, when decks influenced by the Mamluk period between 1250 and 1517 were used. By the time that tradition had migrated to the 'in crowd' of the early 1900s, there were 78 cards in a typical deck, divided into two types: the Major Arcana and the Minor Arcana. The Major is made up of 22 cards – each representing one of a series of key figures (the archetypes): The Empress, The Hierophant and The High Priestess, etc., representing timeless rites of passage of the human condition. The Minor is made up of a further 56 cards, comprising four suits: Cups, Swords, Wands and Pentacles.

Cups associated with emotions
Swords associated with intellect
Wands associated with drive and creativity
Pentacles associated with material world, work and money

In Pamela's tarot designs there's an abundance of nature references: streams for the ceaseless movement of time . . . a sense of journey in mountains, harvest, hills, flowers such as sunflowers (symbolising exuberance and joy), pomegranates symbolising fertility and perhaps hinting at the cross-cultural reference of pomegranates in the folklore of Judaism where each seed is mentioned as a representation of divine law, or ancient Persia where the fruit was associated with beauty, or Greece where it represents links between the living and the dead, or Islamic scripture where it lands as the fruit of paradise.

The deck, published in 1909, is still the most widely used in the world today and is still called the 'Rider-Waite deck'. Her iconography and trademark hand-written initials are present on every single card. Despite there being thousands of decks out there, this was one of the first that came into the mainstream because of its ease of use. Each picture connected and held a remarkable number of clues to its meaning and expansive messages and codes.[3] For her behemoth project – 78 artworks – she was paid a low flat fee. She didn't get royalties.

> Who dares to do anything without fear of what some other will think or say? How can a country, have a living, growing art when it is so bound by fear, the most dreadful of evils?
>
> This marvellous, great country, big in all its feeling and full of energy and yet producing almost no freedom of thought or work!
>
> Taken from 'A Protest Against Fear' written in *The Craftsmen* pamphlet in 1907 by Pamela Colman Smith

Pamela lived within the intersections of faith, art and craft and it demanded a huge amount of defiance from her. I'm told regularly that my work is 'risky', a term I associate with fear. It's only through inner work that I'm able to transmute some of the oppressive thoughts about not being good enough . . . Imagine if I was able to call Pixie! I feel her staunch and honest punk spirit would have got me through many a sticky psychological situation.

Ritual, practice, meditation, stillness-in-thought: each brings my body and mind home, offers me anchors and respect for inhabiting faith and releasing fear as a concept. I have a responsibility to believe in hope and to believe that some wishes may just come true, without always being able to explain why. I believe in love, and how it occurs unexpectedly with such purpose and emergence. I believe that life can be better even when I'm consumed by sorrow. And, though I'm shy to admit it for fear of the hawk-eyed sceptic . . . I know that if I believe in love, I believe in magic on occasion too, because they are interchangeable.

The action of shuffling a deck of tarot cards, especially in our fragmented, device-dependent age, is a soothing, mesmeric act, in the way that magic often is. Working with tarot cards to learn about alternative guidance, I've found to be firstly, fun and also beautiful.

I started reading tarot when I started to learn about Pixie, as though she was giving me permission through her artwork to defy science. Pamela's cards are designed as a divine invitation to understand more about a situation. The cards encompass life's light and shadow. It's important to note that tarot cards act as an unlocking of inner power and knowing within you, rather than simply and straight-forwardly foretelling the future. The Death card for example, means 'an ending' rather than literal loss of life.

Pamela's deck communicates the theme of each card through her images, making them far more accessible than previous tarots. She changed the game and had fun with it, imprinting herself on every card with her snake-shaped initials acting as a signature on the artwork. She nodded to her friends by drawing them into the designs. The white dog on The Fool card is said to have belonged to Edie Craig, who was Ellen Terry's daughter and a great friend of Pamela's.

So much of Pamela's work has been lost, and rumour has it that you can come across some of her artwork sold as bric-a-brac in the Bude area of Cornwall, where she spent her old age with views of the sea and lived with a woman called Nora Lake, whom she affectionately nicknamed 'moley', who many think was her lover.

Imagine stumbling across one of her pieces. My dream.

Pamela's independence and rebel nature have inspired a freedom and ambiguity in my own life. She's helped me escape the discomfort of shapeshifting for the sake of pleasing everyone but myself. There are many things, for example, I could do to increase the traffic on my social media accounts that I'm told would make me 'more marketable'. There are people, companies, producers and commissioners I could meet or re-meet for me to pitch streams of ideas for content, programmes, campaigns, series . . . There are so many more parties and events I could be attending to create networks that would 'better' my position in the hierarchy of celebrity. There are different ways I could do my hair. There are techniques out there to reduce the lines on my face, the same lines that prove I'm getting older and becoming less 'relevant' in the eyes of modern beauty standards. I've experienced the expectation to not be on my own side so many times, but I choose to move through and grow with intuition, listening to the warning signs of bodily aches when I'm in places or navigating spaces that aren't meant for me. I'd rather try new things, discover new parts of myself and explore prospects in uncharted territory than work for an institution where I can feel so unwanted that I have a headache.

You get the sense that 'living a life on one's own terms' was Pamela's life-force and it's gutting to think how some of her struggles still apply today.

> It's still a struggle, right? For people who do not fit into society's preconceived boxes, right? Pamela, I feel like she pushed

> and pushed and tried and tried, her letters at certain junctures of her life are so heartbreaking because she's so frustrated and disappointed by publishers and art dealers who she feels are cheating her. And they probably were. Though she tries to take control of her means of production. She has her own press; she edits and creates her own magazine; she tries to do her own fine art exhibitions; she independently gives performances that she's writing, directing and performing herself. But consistently and repeatedly every time she tries to go beyond . . . she's reduced, and it's both so exemplary about what women, especially non-gender-conforming women, can achieve . . .
>
> Elizabeth Foley O'Connor, author of *Pamela Colman Smith: Artist, Feminist & Mystic*, on her experience of researching Pamela Colman Smith.

Much of Pamela's multidisciplinary portfolio was created over decades – including creating her own literary zine called *The Green Sheaf*. She designed detailed costumes for touring shows, making puppets, performing theatre, engaging in esotericism, and even adding her voice to the suffrage movement. Her archive is impressive and her impact should be recognised. On the one hand, she has been immortalised through her physical deck of cards, which has passed through the hands of witches,[4] soothsayers and fortune tellers the world over for over a hundred years. But her name remains out of sight. So I'm asking myself, the scholar, and anyone else inquisitive out there to go on the journey . . . to find the signs and meanings in her art that affect our present.

January 2024

Cartagena, Colombia

Dear Pixie

I read tarot over dinner tonight, among the trees, for an incredible artist and designer who is 61 and would like to find romance. We talk about a lot, eye to eye. We are on an island called Tierra Bomba, a kilometre off the coast of Cartagena in the Caribbean Sea. We speak about the state of the world, how people are questioning the ways things have always been. She is very beautiful with raven hair and the eyes of worlds. She travelled alone on her sixty-first birthday to have a reset, to envisage the year ahead of her and work out how to bring the right kind of romance into her life after having been single for 15 years. She tells me how she left Iran when she was 15 years old and heard the call of the United States of America, where she ended up refreshed by the luscious greens of Seattle. She's funny and wise and kind and I'm trying not to show I'm super concentrating as I want her to gain something from the reading, which means a combination of my 'go-to' – which is chatting away, asking questions, giggling, and in contrast to the fear of magic, not taking things too seriously. I've found in the learning of reading tarot there's a calm available, different to an adrenaline-spiking giddiness, a social mode I've tapped into most of my life, something about 'entertaining' // people pleasing // performance. I know you designed this very deck I use, but did you read yourself?

The Sisterhood is in motion again. After the reading, I'm wondering if my new friend thinks I'm mad, in the same way the other tourists sitting around drinking rosé and looking at their phones probably do. Instead, she says, 'But how!? How! How out of all of these cards did the right ones know to find me and answer my specific question on love?' I reply, 'I don't know, maybe because you are open to it?'

I want to thank you, Pixie, for the persistence in soul connection, in all you created, blessing all our imaginations with abundant fuel

Gemma Xx

Faith, a comforting space to hold?

The irreconcilable abuse of power that has been exposed in religious institutions throughout history has me resonating with the distrust and outrage many feel towards faith.

I have only ever been to church with my lovely dad who has been a member of the Pentecostal Church, as many Jamaican people his age are, since he was born. Going into a place where you're so unconditionally welcomed has always taken my breath away, and I've always felt the atoms of my soul flow with joy when everyone sings together. I've been curious about the rapture of spirit from a young age. I remember being no older than nine or 10 and asking if I could be one of the churchgoers to stay behind at one service to see if 'the spirit would visit me' and I was told yes, so I waited my turn (I was the youngest person in line) for an elder to put their hand on my shoulder and invite god in. I was a bit scared, but mostly fascinated. I watched the people in front of me burst into tears, and jolt their bodies. I didn't cry or convulse like some of the grown-ups did, but I remember feeling pleased about such unusual behaviour being so seemingly rational and important to the adults.

On The Sacred

We're not sold solemnity, peace, prayer or pilgrimage as a value worth holding onto or trying to achieve nowadays. But solemnity has offered me a profound sense of self at pivotal points in my life. I once hiked to the bottom of Malawi's highest waterfall to find children backflip on repeat among the waters. For them it was everyday play; no phones, just freedom in the most divine surroundings – for me it was proof that Eden is a real place.

Another time I unexpectedly stirred from my womb and my gut as I trekked to the top of Mount Kenya. Laughter began to carry me forward as it felt there wasn't much fear left to hold on to, on that morning as we reached the summit, head torches lighting our scrambles for the right footing at over 16,000 feet. All we knew is that we were putting our fate in the hands of the patient mountain and it brought my body to release in pure unfiltered giggles for the absurdity of it all. Perhaps a similar emotion to what I witnessed in church that day, as a child in search of spirit.

I think we can make holy journeys of the mind, too, without going too physically far, in the dignity offered by visual art, the colour we paint our walls, the aesthetic we nurture, watching performance among audiences in the dark, taking solo time to flick through poetry books – all of it can tempt a visit from something outside of us, all of it can offer places to put our soul-anchors, ground our potential for respect, hope and belief.

A Sense Memory: Amelia[5]

Los Angeles 2023

I talk with my friend Amelia one unforgettable afternoon infused with the feeling that the Immortal Sisterhood is close and how the act of its construction is changing me. I explain the work of writing this book, how it comes through me and acts as a physical catharsis because of how interlinked so much of it seems, the coincidences and topsy-turvy happenings, and how it's always been like that for me since the genesis of this book. How my dreams have sometimes occurred as predictions and visions, even as far back as when I was a child.

The picturesque Californian hills, the faded glamour of a distant, too familiar HOLLYWOOD sign seen from a deck in

Echo Park, East-Central Los Angeles. I've always loved forming new friendships and bonds and am spilling all the beans of hopes and dreams. Amelia and I are chatting and chatting and chatting like there's no tomorrow, talking about our life experiences, art and the planet. When we move onto the topic of complicated families, I try to steady myself against the shame that stirs in my lower back and the fog that wraps around my brain when I talk about how delicate a particular family relationship is. How much it hurts sometimes, and how rather than curdle in blame my heart just wants familial love and radical care.

Here I am, a sunshine-chasing runaway in Cali, and I'm here to connect, to continue to do some research for wanderlust and writing and do some exploring of new and brave friendships. The calendar and this trip were also quietly working in cahoots, and I realise I'm also there to reflect and to listen to the shared journeys of grief around the anniversary of a friend dying, nearly to the day, three years previously. The very same friend I made my first trip to the bonkers city of Los Angeles with, when we were brighter, younger things in 2011. During that trip, we were buoyed by hysterical joy, she got tattooed and we threw ourselves into the alien planet of LA lifestyle. I remember being afraid to be led by the neon lights of PSYCHICS & CLAIRVOYANCE that were on every street corner, but my dear friend was all for it. 'You'll get the job,' I remember one particular pirate-like fortune teller proclaimed to me, as we were lured into a conversation that was essentially a sales pitch on a boulevard in Venice Beach. 'You,' said our 'all-knowing' real-life **Zoltar**, as he wryly turned in my direction, and I remembered I didn't want to be told what would happen in my future. But here we were, on my first trip to LA, with my high-flying, incredible friend, about to hang out on Venice Beach like in the movies, and a caricature of a fortune teller had accosted us, telling us that we wouldn't even need to pay if we didn't want to . . . he just had to tell us our 'futures' because they were so available to him. 'You . . . well . . . I know something . . .' he said so compellingly that I forgot all about my decision not to hear anything about my future.

'You're bisexual,' he said and that was it.

Here I was, back in LA all these years later, and on an outdoor deck, overlooking the zooming freeway, this time with my friend, wonderful Amelia. We've eaten some chocolate sprinkled with mushrooms, and birds circle above us. We spot multiple red-tailed hawks almost summoning us and woodpeckers making music in trees so much taller than I'm used to. I'm hazy from the hills and the sunshine I had been starved of in Scotland and the chocolate with the mushrooms and it's all these years later and I've lost my friend who I first visited with. I'll never know why life is cruel enough for such tragedy. But, entwined with the grief I'm in, I'm in love with friendships that are new and coincidences and the freedom I feel viscerally reverberate through me and our hive when we travel in love. I see it there: a red-tailed hawk circling above our heads.

Entangled & Embodied

As womxn who play the heavily loaded game called The Entertainment Industry, we so often become beholden to 'the man' / a brutalism that sits comfortably on a throne of power. We can become squashed, moulded and contorted by gatekeepers / 'markers of success' that don't want to factor in the emotional nature of our careers. Appearance / conformity, the didacticism of oligarch-run media . . . If anything, the more we try to 'play the game' in duality of displaying any sign of vulnerability or need for tenderness, support or empathy, the more pressure there is for us to harden and take whatever may be harming us 'on the chin'. But I will never escape or silence the loss of Caroline and all she went through preceding her death, nor Amy's for that matter. Both, despite only having a personal relationship with one of them and the other – **parasocial** / threaded in connection by my fandom and our mutual gravitation towards certain folk and exciting places to hang out and partake in encouraged revelry in London during a certain time. Caroline Flack and Amy Winehouse's tragic deaths have stained the narratives of British celebrity and more deeply still our society's conditioned normalisation of a de-humanising 'take-down' that occurs . . . when we don't question the way in which we watch a young woman in danger and still demand perfection. We scrutinise, troll and gossip about them instead, even when we know in our guts they are being exploited and abandoned by any kind of nurture or time for repair, when they are openly losing a grip on health or reality. We want famous womxn to stay palatable, likeable and in a kind of perceived optimum (unrealistic) girl / womanhood as a deflection from a system that we know makes it impossible.

how

can

we

support

all

womxn?

Cuckoo

& still the hawk flies above. I look up the esoteric symbolism of a red-tailed hawk and the word 'determination' comes up, which makes me even headier: so often I feel the need for determination but fold in fear of being hurt and pushed off track. The word 'love' comes up in the research: love in the position it holds in friend and family entanglements, and how potent true forgiveness can be. And 'protection': some believe the bird is a sign that an angel is watching over you.

Amelia and I spend hours like teenagers, sharing our desires and dreams and playing each other songs – jaunty folk music, the metaphysical lyrics of Erykah Badu, the honeyed melodies of D'Angelo or drum-beats from Zimbabwe – it all has us forgetting about the treacherous whirr of the space-ship-style cars on the freeway below. We stop squinting to just about make out the almost haunting HOLLYWOOD sign in the distance and create a new paradigm for an evening. I teach Amelia the 'breath of fire' from my yoga practice and for the first time in a long time, I don't have to add the eye-roll of faux cynicism when I talk about my hobbies and wishes at the risk of them being too 'woo woo' or 'child-like' or 'unrealistic'. It's such a fun and beautiful, rare afternoon . . . We cry together in commemoration of our heartbreaks and loves no longer. I express how I feel an important yearning to hold a positive outlook, and together we imagine the symbiosis that is possible between joy and pain, humans and nature, past and future, truth and imagination, vision and reality, and we dance on the potency of pure and unapologetic hope all day.

I've found hope in the catharsis and bond of friendship. When you get to scream TRUTH. When it doesn't matter if it makes total sense / when you haven't been 'the perfect woman' but you have love for one another all the same.

Reading, sometimes meditation, sometimes prayer, the act of imagination and creation, asking what might seem like silly or unusual questions (sometimes on repeat), writing and listening, choosing who to listen to, much unlearning: it has all ensued / a fever dream.

The result right now is that I will hold my head high in the face of oppression, and I will not stand for the harm we face as a sisterhood, a coven, an identity. We seem to be eviscerated so easily, and yet in contrast tethered together so strongly by our ability to overcome and synchronise despite our differences . . . come back from the shadows and resist. As I carousel into my fourth decade, I don't give a fuck so much about being deemed 'suitable' or 'good enough' for anyone's brief but my own, in a world where womxn deserve better access to the truth we hold in our bodies and how it responds to what's around us, from plants to the moon. We are works of nature and I love us for our nuance, our mystery and complexity. We are as powerful as The Waves and I thank Pixie (& Amelia & Caroline & California) for showing me that.

Faith as a craft worth studying?

There is no through-line, one straight, explainable strategy or path if you're someone who hears 'I can't quite place you' as many times as I have. But I don't desire to be 'placed' and I definitely am not in the slightest bit interested in staying in 'my' lane. I can't bear the reductiveness of becoming just one 'type of person' for ever. Think of Wang, whose academic prowess made her top of the astronomy field in Ancient China. Not only was this beyond any expectation for a woman, she shapeshifted into democratising education overall, wrote poetry when she was angry and dismayed, and learned horse riding with her best friend. Her life was full of the rich qualities and range not expected of women. It's part of all our liberation beyond sex, beyond race, beyond silos, beyond past compromise.

Reactions hang in the air when people find my changing choices of image, career, and creative expression too 'different' to what they would do. When my eyes are met with confusion / suspicion or plain bewilderment, in these moments, I'm aware of how damaging that can be if I internalise this feeling of not being heard or seen.

Let's not limit our journeys to lanes or advise anyone else to do so unsolicited. I'd love for us all to remember that choices are precious acts of living and that we should encourage ourselves and others to make them with heart, instinct and variety. That way, our openness to difference could transform a society that's scrabbling to 'fit in' but still feeling so lonely. It's very easy for my existence to feel ironic and strange a lot of the time. Cosmological paradigms away from the British mantra 'Keep Calm and Carry On' – it's more 'keeping chaotic but staying grounded'.

I'm unsurprised Pamela was drawn to esoteric practice and faith. Like magpies, we weirdos and wanderers are attracted to thought outside of logic. But it's not just Pamela's seemingly clairvoyant association that intrigues me the most; it's her process that I want to know about. I get the feeling that she didn't suffer fools lightly. Many are fascinated by the fact she joined the Hermetic Order of The Golden Dawn, which she was introduced to by her friend, Irish poet and occultist William Butler

Yeats, sometime during her twenties. But what fascinates me the most is that she got out, decided to leave, and eventually ended up practicing Christianity. Because adventurous weirdos want and need flow, and so they need the grit and the resilience to do what's right for them at any given moment; they're open to change their minds, bodies, souls and, in this case, beliefs.

I feel awe every time I see the interconnections between the members of The Sisterhood and their experiences . . . Women who choose poetry as a form of expression, for example. Wang Zhenyi and Una Marson (see p.43) both knew the power available to them by weaving poetic form into other things they were known for. Both showed that if you believe in equality, words and their creative formation are a worthwhile labour. What would they have been like to talk to about this chosen act? In a world where we're often encouraged as women to squash 'big feelings' down for want of being considered 'nice' / 'ladylike' or 'demure', does calling shit out on paper make us feel better? I for one sure as hell think: yes. I have been afraid of my anger my whole life and now, in my fortieth year, I wield metaphors and worship the feeling that of all the things I've lost, such as the robustness of youth, I have and will always have a deep love of writing, as a form of resistance against oppression and a way out of the silence.

Chapter Threads

Arthur Ransome – English author, intelligence agent and journalist.

Bohemia in London – a non-fiction title written by Arthur Ransome.

fae – alternative word for fairy.

aural-heart-lines – spoken wisdom that travels.

Pratt Institute – founded in 1887, The Pratt Institute is a prestigious university in Brooklyn, New York known for delivering some of the best higher education in art, design and architecture.

Bram Stoker – Irish novelist and theatre boss, who famously wrote *Dracula*.

William Butler Yeats – poet and former senator of the Irish Free State.

Ellen Terry – English Theatre Actor / Performer.

synaesthesia – a neurological condition in which stimulation of one sensory pathway leads to automatic, involuntary experiences in a second sensory pathway.

Hermetic Order of The Golden Dawn – a secret society founded in the late nineteenth century devoted to the study of Western esotericism, Egyptian magic, tarot and astrology.

Yemanja – Orisha (deity) in Yoruba religion, associated with the ocean, motherhood and feminine power.

Kemet – ancient name for Egypt, meaning 'the Black Land'

Zoltar – a machine operated fortune teller, from the movie *Big*, with Tom Hanks from 1988.

parasocial – word of the year in 2025, meaning to overly relate or identify with someone, usually via their public persona.

3

Una Marson

The broadly casting poet

'I am black and so I must be more clever than white folk.'

Una Marson, 'The Black Burden', from her poetry collection *The Moth and the Star*, 1937

Born: 6 February 1905, Santa Cruz, Jamaica
Died: 6 May 1965, Kingston, Jamaica
Sign: Aquarius
Pronouns: She / Her

Una Marson was an OUTSTANDING sister. Born in the St Elizabeth parish of Jamaica in 1905, she became the first Black woman to both present and produce on the BBC.

It seems her heart was wide open from a young age. When her middle-class family fell upon hard times, they moved from the countryside – where she'd studied at private school and had become an avid reader of the available literature, mostly English classic titles – to the capital, Kingston. Her education abruptly stopped, but she worked as a volunteer social worker, gaining in-depth knowledge of people of all classes, and developed empathy for the lives of those struggling in 1920s Jamaica – still 40 years away from achieving independence from the UK.

Una, like many others in this hood, had a creative practice and skillset that spanned disciplines. By the age of 21 she was the first female editor and publisher of a monthly political journal – *The Jamaica Critic*. But this was just the beginning. Two years later she established her own magazine about women's economic and cultural status called *The Cosmopolitan*. For the next few years, alongside editing her own magazine, she was a regular contributor to many of Jamaica's most esteemed publications, including *The Daily Gleaner* and *The Jamaica Standard*, and also found time to have two of her poetry collections published. By 1932, her play, *At What A Price*, was staged at Ward Theatre in Kingston. All this by the age of just 27.

Wanderlust and ambition brought Marson to the heart of the imperial rule she saw playing out on her own island, with her move to London in 1932. Reading her work from that time, I'm enthralled by how she describes the atmosphere of the United Kingdom through the gaze of a young, politicised Jamaican woman.

I am black
And so I must be
More clever than white folk,
More wise than white folk,
More discreet than white folk,
More courageous than white folk . . .
I am black,
And I have got to travel
Even farther than white folk,
For time moves on –
I must not laugh too much,

> They say black folk can only laugh . . .
>
> From 'Black Burden' by Una Marson, 1937

Her work suggests she felt like an outsider and frequently experienced racism. And yet she continued to pioneer and use her voice on both sides of the Atlantic. I find the duality in how she did that so inspiring and impressive. On one hand, actively campaigning by joining the likes of organisations and collectives such as **The League of Coloured Peoples** and speaking at high-profile events such as the International Alliance of Women for Suffrage and Legal Citizenship in Istanbul in 1935. On the other hand, channelling her opinions and experiences through literature and the arts. Her plays were put on in London, but her roots took her work back to Jamaica. Her play *London Calling* was staged at the Ward Theatre in Kingston in 1937, exploring sexual politics in a patriarchal society and satirising colonial policy. Her non-conformism was also reflected in her use of language, darting from Patois to formal English, depending on the form her writing was to take.

Sister Synchronicity: WordPLAY

I've come to learn that if you have mixed heritage, as so many of us do, in the world right now, those different parts of ourselves can at first seem in conflict with each other. But if we are able to embrace them, then we are able to feel at home in our minds and bodies and perhaps more in what I can only describe as an abstract sense of place, rather than locating ourselves in specificity, especially when it comes to colonial language. Is sunshine home to me? Yes. Is the sea home to me? Yes, but only in certain seasons. Phases, changes in the atmosphere, temperature and self, all the senses from sound to the smell of salted air, or sun baked rock against skin can all bring me home wherever I may be.

I spoke with a steward of Irish culture not long ago, who told me that when she began to learn the traditional Irish language she began to de-shackle herself mentally from an 'English properness' that she'd felt a duty to uphold all her life until her forties. She loosened her control on formal learning and phonetics and began to learn sayings and words from her own land. She spoke of noticing how much more wild she looked when she watched herself on videos of her speaking in her original mother tongue. How powerful and wild and free our ancestors might have been, I thought.

Ubuntu

I try sometimes not to be too self-conscious of my aural expression but to see what comes out when I'm genuinely responding to an atmosphere or place or feeling or particular person or audience. I was born in Birmingham, in the middle of England, in the middle of the 1980s, and even though we moved when I was two, it's when I'm there that I can hear a Brum-flavoured bounce roll off my tongue quite inexplicably. I lived in London for many years, first South, then I moved out to the Home Counties, then back to London, this time East, and then Margate, and from there I can charge the reserves of my cockney-street-mash-up of slang, like armour when I need it in sketchy or comical situations. I now live in Scotland, where I hear my grandad's vernacular in Glasgow. All these linguistic experiences help me to understand myself, just like I recognise some of the elegant phrases in Africa or the twangs of verbosity and joy in some of the voices of African Americans, and I'm humbled by the fusions of references in Caribbean Island voices.

Ubuntu is a philosophy on interconnectedness that originated in South Africa. It's structured on collective thinking over the centring of the individual and includes components of restorative justice only being truly achieved in unity.

Una spent a lifetime dedicated to using her voice as a feminist, activist, poet, producer, playwright and journalist – another polymath in our midst. She fought for platforms to express progressive ideas around decolonising relations between Europe, the Caribbean and Africa. She published academic theory and words on the themes of nature, love and sexuality through poetry. She, of course, also travelled the world doing so.

Echoes and ripples

Una was a **Pan-Africanist,** a philosophy that shaped much of her broadcast and academic work.

In **Imaobong Umoren**'s paper 'This is the Age of Woman: Black Feminism and Black Internationalism', there's a chapter about the works of Una Marson from 1928 to 1938. It cites scholar Brent Hayes Edwards's book; *The Practice of Diaspora*[1] here:

> Marson's black feminism was also linked to black internationalism. As a political philosophy, black internationalism promoted black self-determination and sought to create links between different black populations around the world.

She goes on to state how publishing and academia have a responsibility to hold Black women writers of the past, such as Una, in high esteem. This has a beneficial ripple effect in our collective sense that all women are worth hearing from and have a chance to feel galvanised and worthy of producing work. If we are lucky enough to travel we should take the books of Black women writers wherever we go, and if we're able to pass them on, I believe we should.

The right words, when read at exactly the right time, can act as radical open arms / a safety / threads in a tapestry of literary offerings when written in such ways as Una Marson used them. Una knew the importance of words spoken and **cast broadly** in the act of 'broad-cast' and in the form of poetry. It feels when reading her work like it was cultivated language that came with ease to her, a practice of honouring one's emotion with beat and irreverence for writing and speaking.

Think not that those who spend their time
In building up the lofty rhyme
Are often of another clime
Than those who pass them by.
They differ not but in degree:-
More deeply feel all that they see.
They hold to nature the great key,
And ope' the portals wide.
What some will pass and scarce admire
Just sets the poet's soul afire;
In praise of it he ne'er can tire,
In rapture he is lost.
He knows that many hearts are sad
That need someone to make them glad;
They would be happy if they had
A sympathising friend.
His poet's heart goes out to these,
Their sorrows and their woes he sees
By words of comfort oft he frees
The weary burdened heart.

From 'The Poet's Heart' by Una Marson, self-published in 1930 as part of *Tropic Reveries.*

As someone who has had to defend my use of colloquial language – something I feel as very Jamaican – over the years of growing up in England, I find it refreshing to read the richness of culture in Marson's work. I'm in awe of the drive and sheer quantity of multidisciplinary work she produced. And she didn't let the Second World War stop her. She kept globetrotting throughout the 1930s, setting up Jamaica's first Save the Children fund en route, as well as becoming a producer of an important BBC Radio show, *Calling The West Indies*, in 1939, a show in which West Indian troops on active service read letters to their loved ones back home across the Caribbean.

A Sense Memory: Discipline

***A young woman** *of 25 has her dream job. She's a radio presenter. She gets to talk, giggle, connect and play music to the masses for a living. She can hardly believe her luck. After a few years making her mark in her early twenties on a specialist, less-widely listened-to station, she gets a promotion to one of the biggest broadcasting networks in the world. The lights around this promotion are dazzling, and she strides headily towards what she's told will be 'success'. She's bold in her pursuit, she's loud, she's proud, she's alternative and she thinks it gives her a uniqueness that might be rewarded if she works hard enough, and is at least safe. She bats away impostor syndrome and intrusive negative impostor-like stirrings with a devotion to fun and sparkle and living in each moment as though it could be her last. She becomes used to the stars, she interviews people in POP and Hollywood types, and basks in the glow of precious and fast situations that will make wonderful anecdotes in the pub. One morning Whoopi Goldberg comes into her radio studio and asks to borrow the cocoa butter belonging to a producer that's propped up on the side. The warmth is magnetic that morning and the young* *radio presenter falls in a quick familial kind of love with Whoopi. She asks her if she'll be her 'honorary Grandma' and Whoopi says yes. The young radio presenter with the world at her feet lights up from the inside; she's never really had a grandma figure in her life until now . . . The presenter's childhood before her big break had been dappled with neglect, unidentified racism and an inexplicable search for the healing found in escapist optimism, the arts and an innocent belief in the good in humanity. She is now 25, an adult, she thinks. She's made it. She has the dream job and it feels exactly that; a dream in which she flies . . . she ignores a low buzz she hears in the air from time to time / a repression of when she was told she would struggle in life and that she's of unfortunate stock / a problem child in a world full of problems. Instead she says yes to everything: every dancefloor, every outrageous creative idea, challenge, meeting, job, campaign and potentially exciting friendship. She adjusts her rose tinted glasses with sleek professionalism whenever she notes the similarities in the gatekeepers, the people in charge of what she gets paid and who advise or brief her in each given situation to bend a little more 'that way', or shift a bit 'this way',* or *be 'more like', or speak 'more like', and that she must use her energy and potential for the 'likes' and POPularity and palatability that are part of the winning formula of working 'in media' . . . the creative 'industries' . . . She wades through the layers of keeping up with what's relevant, with attractiveness, with being young and cool and white-schmoking-hot, and tries to learn at different levels of the game, but is often confused by many of the discoveries or secrets or designer outfits, glitz and free wine. Sometimes she slips upon snakes while looking for the next set of ladders. Climbing ladders in eight-inch heels is a tiring pursuit, she learns. But she is only 25. She wins awards for projects and radio and is recognised for the amount of spaces she is able to shapeshift to fit into.*

A Sense Memory: It's different here

'*The thing is Gemma, it's different here you see . . .*' I was told while sitting in an office made of glass walls over a small corporate-grey desk made of hard plastic. I had been called into an unexpected – but seemingly important – meeting with middle management of a well-known broadcasting network. I had just landed a promotion and was hosting a show on a 'bigger network' with more listeners than before. I was chuffed and I thought things were going well. I was, in this meeting, more curious rather than afraid. I was working in an industry after all that created worlds within the world, one where every meeting with a boss felt disproportionately important as we were, in fact, not performing brain surgery. I was a broadcaster providing a 'public service', so it was imperative that the 'public' had access to tell me not only how I did my job, but how I conducted elements of my personality. We were aware that our jobs were sought after, unique and therefore very difficult, required limitless talent and skill, and that this included likability. One of my skills had to be being liked by as many people as possible.

You could get a call any moment of any day to tell you that your fate was changing . . . You were being posted to another show, perhaps one with hours that would change your life and reshape your mental health (I did six years of breakfast radio shows, and during the height of my radio career, I was on air from 4.00–6.30 a.m. Monday to Friday) / perhaps your show would be broadcast in another city entirely? As presenters we were kept on our toes. There I was, at a peak moment, on the snazzy 'big' station, where stars languished on office chairs in studios and Britpop rock 'n' roll legends held sway with an ego-defining gravity that had us see them as a kind of royalty. As the meeting started to unfold, it became clear that this was going be an appraisal, or some kind of reprimanding? I'm not sure I'll have the right language for what transpired even to this day.

For the next hour, I was talked through a paper flip chart depicting a particular market research tool I'd never been introduced to before, despite having worked for the organisation for years. This 'system', I was told, was used weekly to gauge the 'temperature' of the listeners' response to my work. Step by step, it was outlined how I had been 'failing' in my new role on the 'bigger station'. At one point, which I'll never forget, my name was in the middle of a piece of paper with larger and smaller words around it, to describe specific feedback about my style of presentation . . . 'annoying' and 'loud' were two that I remember; I've blocked out the others. I was in shock. I was then told the complicated scoring part of this 'market research' I'd never heard of and that I was coming in 'off a few points' in every show to keep listeners happy.

'But what do I need to change?' I asked, bewildered by the entire experience.

'Well, things are a bit different here . . . You perhaps need to tone it down a bit on this new station . . . Perhaps laugh a bit less.'

Up STAND

The reputation of being a British broadcaster on the BBC, to 'cast broadly' and dependably, 'be understood by many'/ a pillar of upstanding 'Britishness', is an aspiration that's a little intimidating if you're not in the royal family or from aristocracy, but poignant and impactful for many the world over all the same.

I once lived in a wild house share in Dalston, East London, where odd art was everywhere, including a giant raised frame as you came up the stairs that was filled with cigarettes butts (as art). I lived in the only room painted white, which was the attic room, and you had to climb a ladder to get to. I came down one night to tell some of my flatmates who were listening to techno music really loudly in the kitchen to turn it down and tried to explain that I had a radio show early in the morning. When one of my flatmate's guests asked me what station I worked for, I told her that I worked for the BBC and she burst into tears. She went on to explain that she had grown up in the dictatorship in Chile and that the BBC World Service had been her only access to outside news. Another time when a woman once told me that her mixed race three-year-old daughter had run towards the telly when I was presenting Glastonbury one year, and started touching the screen and cheering because she saw someone like her on the TV, it humbled me. I was willing to be twisted into any shape, cookie-cut, trained and critiqued if I could become great at my craft and have a life of service broadcasting.

There is no belonging like the connection felt when on live radio. I'm yet to find a more powerful way to feel as together with the people, all of us – flesh, bones, fragile (and stronger together when in unison) in comparison to the magic of waves – in the same moment and necessity for small daily joys and nourishment. The magic of live radio will never be overriden by AI or even podcasts.

Marson carried a mission of public integration and Black nationalism through everything she did. Her work was often beautiful and multiform, imbuing politics, humour and philosophical thinking into plays, articles, poetry, public speaking and broadcasting. Over the years, her work was commended by **George Orwell.** Her show *Calling The West Indies*, which later evolved into *Caribbean Voices* for the World Service, lasted until 1958. She released an abundance of poetry, travelled as a public speaker between the US, the Caribbean, the UK and Israel. But her personal life and mental health suffered as a result of tirelessly going around the world to push against the patriarchy and racism.

Imagine being Black, a woman, empathetic, clever, unmarried, not formally educated, and determined. Now, imagine being all that in the West in the 1930s, 1940s and 1950s.

A Sense Memory: Sleepy, jolly, clown

One morning during a daily stint of hosting a live breakfast radio show (a vocation that requires constant improvisation), when I was in my early twenties, I remember being set a challenge on air to 'recreate' a moment from a popular TV Show that was on at the time, one of those episodic modelling contests, *Project Runway*, or *Britain's Next Top Model*, I can't remember which. The on-air challenge? Well, I had half an hour to head out of the studio with a digital camera and recreate the photoshoot challenge the shows's contestants had done the night before. This was different, though: this was satire, this was a chance to play into the delirium and the absurdity of everything – the fashion industry, the seriousness of it – and to subvert the 'sexiness' that the male gaze so often bestowed upon us. I was comfortable with our listeners. Our mornings felt like a gang of friends having a laugh. The only thing dividing us really was the fact that we were the ones that actually pressed play on the songs that we all loved listening to. This was during the years that I fell in love with the medium of radio, and my love affair with the quality of jolly power was still fresh. I enjoyed shocking my older co-host, who I saw as an uncle-like figure and enjoyed taunting, often by playing the clown to his smooth seamlessness. So I decided to recreate the theme in the short time I had and with no resources (no hair and makeup team, no props, just like on the TV show!) I had to shoot these pics while adding a 'breakfast' theme to the whole thing. I remember being in the staff room, pulling my top down to reveal bare shoulders and smothering my décolletage with cold porridge, trying to poke fun at the common imagery of a woman being 'sexy' but disturbed, with smeared lipstick or sweet food glazed onto their skin. It was 2008 and the 'running-with-wolves' style, wild-eyed, bed-hair and puppy eyes merged with troubling Lolita tropes and heroin chic were still huge trends in the 2000s. I was punk and a radio clown with clumpy bits of oats instead of twinkles in my eyes, looking like I'd been 'pied' or 'gunged' in the same way so many characters were for comedy in 1990s kids TV shows!

Little did I know how much the images were going to look like I had been sick all over myself. The on-air, quickly thought-out challenge went down like a lead balloon. I thought it was so much funnier than it was received. But one of the joys of live breakfast radio was the momentum. If 'banter' or an idea didn't land, you moved on real quick, with no time to let the embarrassment set in. It was more the hate mail that I'd receive on a blue moon that triggered some negative thinking about myself. 'You're a disgrace to other young Black girls, for the way you wear your hair'; 'You're not Black enough for this station'; 'Your speech impediment is distracting' – to name but a few.

A Sense Memory: The Presenter Years: 2008–2024

Being a 'presenter' / labelled as 'talent' is an unusual job. It meant I got to meet countless people and travel all over, which is everlastingly enriching for a sponge like me, but what were the tolls? . . . Because no reality is perfect, even if you present otherwise, and being a professional 'extrovert' was a one-way ticket to exhaustion, especially knowing what I do now about my ability to spend my life as adrenalised and in as high-octane situations as possible. This, combined with the childhood I had, was a potential recipe for some harsh repercussions. Now I'm grown, I can more clearly understand my persistent people-pleasing ways – it was both a psychological and physical pursuit for survival – I hosted years of breakfast shows, forcing my tired body awake before most, except for a usually male cab driver whose car smelled of overworked and overwrought late-night hours. I had such respect for the listeners at those times – it felt like only heroes could be awake in the hours between 4 and 6 a.m., like mothers breastfeeding, paramedics saving lives, people heroically taking themselves on deserved holidays, or those feeding animals on farms. It's also a job that doesn't come with a handbook or particular training. I just did it– whirred and worked away like a dervish who'd been offered a fun job. I learned to 'drive the desk', a radio term for essentially pressing all the buttons and steering the ship, and was so proud of myself: I'd grown up without having enough money in our house and now needed to keep up with the rising rents of an ever-industrialised and luxurious London, and now I wasn't. I was somebody, and I cared about my audience.

I used to spend a lot of time on my own then, travelling from place to place, studio to studio for work. Countless hotel rooms to warrior paint my face to host awards ceremonies for big companies. I have the route from north to south Britain / Brexit Island – embedded in my cells – curling up like an animal on hot trains to prepare for a stint of the graveyard shift on radio. I have to separate and untangle my fear, now that I'll never work in the same way again if I analyse the harder stuff and at the same time reflect in pride for all the beautiful victories, the triumphs and the raw beauty of it all happening for the first time back then, in a life that was being experienced so much more fully than I'd ever thought possible. Life was very different . . . I was young and robust and adrenaline made me love the act of dressing up and going to festivals back then. Unadulterated cackling, the mischief of our youth, when my mates and I travelled for live music, wore uncomfortable garments because in the moment they made us feel better than we did without them, and even took weekends off to go away to crumbling country houses to drink wine and dance in lounges to garage music anarchically. It felt like a time when all of us, societally, looked into one another's eyes from time to time on public transport rather than down into phones.

I was far from lonely. I had interactions with people behind counters in shops and supermarkets. I was paid better for my work when I was young and more conformist and therefore didn't feel guilty about investing in necessary acts of 'holistic balance'. I got massages, went to yoga classes all over the land, and looked up at buildings and architecture because social media didn't saturate time. I felt gloriously anonymous in the human soup at train stations when travelling for work. So much fun was had being a presenter, helter-skeltering about the place to present and converse in studios and on panel chats. I developed a ritual of finding home in my body despite staying in an assortment of mid-level accommodations, I took my favourite tiny trinkets and would always try and get a room with a bath for creature comfort on my own. I didn't have the language or tools for thinking about any kind of neurodivergence. But in hindsight, I was doing so much **masking.**

In Memoriam for Una

In 1961 Una returned to Jamaica for the final time. She died there in 1965, aged 60. As a fan, having read and felt the pain and disappointment in her poetry, I'm left wondering what effect the stress of our workplaces has on our bodies. I know first-hand that can be a blessing and a curse being a woman who intellectually grows in the face of adversity and injustice and then chooses to begin to build the muscle needed to address the lack of representation and diversity. Staying active can be a treacherous journey, one that we are reminded of time and time again in the connected perils of our Sisterhood. But I'm not just here to document hard truths. I want to move through, learn from and most importantly honour the imagination, ingenuity, skill and hubris of the past's trailblazers. In memoriam and picking up the baton all at the same time.

Without Una, I may never have started a career in broadcast at the world's largest public organisation for news, radio, content and television. It was a consortium of radio manufacturers who originated the BBC in 1922 at a critical time in British history in the UK, not long after the First World War. Would it democratise and swing open the door on public truth? Might it perhaps challenge imperialism for the first time? How would the service impact the UK's conditioned imperial psyche? When Una first presented her show – *Caribbean Voices* – in 1943, for example, it may have been the first time many people heard BBC-style **RP** tones mixed with Caribbean Island cadence and inflections. The voice reveals so much. How did the bright tones make the listener feel? How had the very United Kingdom that everyone was listening from influenced people from so far away? How come they were talking of fighting in our wars, putting themselves in harm's way on behalf of 'our queen'? It was the very BBC that cracked open the Pandora's Box on Britain's duty to educate British nations on how such a small part of the world had become so worldly significant. I just wish I could time-travel towards Una. We could grab a coffee in Great Portland Street and I'd endeavour to buy her an Audre Lorde book, one that advocates for the self-care of us and I'm sure you would have your own collection of recommendations too, and unapologetically so. We could share some of the heartache of how the world's most hopeful organisation had let us down, but how conflicted we were sometimes at being so in service of it, and perhaps how our understanding of an evolving civic practice may be a wonderful thing.

November 2025

Royal Infirmary of Edinburgh

Dear Una

I'm writing this from a hospital camp bed after midnight as my daughter has contracted a respiratory virus and has been in hospital while the doctors and nurses check her breathing. My body feels like wreckage and I'm both bewildered by how marvellous the NHS is and staggered by the fact that it still exists. Everyone in here is putting on a brave face, including my baby and me, while they put an inhaler over her mouth. She's strong enough to shake her head and say no, even though she can't talk yet. It's breaking something in me to see her suffering and to only be able to offer her a lap of a ward room with other coughing children and no natural light.

I've been thinking a lot about my identity recently – who I am, how my life has been shaped by my own ambition – but also unquestioning faith. How I'm more politicised than I ever thought I would be, how my heart is in my mouth and how my spine is affected because of uncomfortable sleeps, or watching my daughter recovering from unpleasant symptoms, but knowing that some of the tingles of worry are for the Island of Jamaica right now. It has just been ravaged by a hurricane they are calling Melissa. I'm still trying to understand why so many devastating hurricanes are named after women. Just last year, I was on the phone to my partner's parents finding out about how 'Helene' had swept through their part of North Carolina in the US. Oddly enough, one of the visuals they gave me was describing a caboose that was also home to a community radio station, completely under water, risen from the river opposite. The same radio station I'd hosted an impromptu radio show there, from a very old train carriage, on New Year's Day just a year earlier. It was the sweetest little community radio studio. My way of vibe-checking so many places I've been in the world is to either visit a local radio station or, better still, host a one-off show; I've done this in Paris, New York City, St Lucia, Barbados, Bamako in Mali, Freetown in Sierra Leone and Accra in Ghana. I have lots of joyous memories from doing this, the most ecstatic being when I went to check out a breakfast show in Barbados, and it was such high-energy brilliance in the way all the best Breakfast radio shows should be. I got to enjoy looking through the glass and wandering around the office. I find quiet radio offices, early in the morning, to be more familiar than any boutique hotel. Anyway, I bumped into a woman grooving so hard to her favourite song on the playlist that particular morning with all her might. It took a beat to notice: it was a mop that she had in her hand and was using as a prop to sing along with the words. She was the grooviest office cleaner I've ever come across in my life.

In Jamaica, the land is hurting after the storms, and people are coming together to reset and rebuild.

What was your relationship with the island?

Did you visit anywhere else in the Caribbean?

I know you went to North America to speak about Pan-Africanism. I would be so interested to know more about how that idea was received in the US, during the 1960s? Were there others that looked like you when you travelled?

I'm an activist in many respects too, and a broadcaster also. I've been working for the BBC for many years, where I know you paved the way. I started a vagabond, with no clue but with a mania for culture and an almost teen-like dream for how the power of connection can change the world . . . I realised quickly that live radio was fun, but so much more – also a craft, and one of the most connective acts you could do with lots of people, all at once . . . I let go of my wanting to be an actor (which had been the plan) and threw myself in. I wish I'd been recommended a therapist, though. My constitution was not ready for the male dominance, the ego and the competition.

Every now and then, listeners would send lengthy emails when I was on a station called BBC 1Xtra – which at the time had the tagline 'Love Black Music, Love 1Xtra' – stating how I wasn't 'Black enough' for the station. But the will and exhilaration overrode the criticism back then. I was 23.

How did you do it? With so much scrutiny from a listening nation?

I have to go now, as they need to check my daughter again. But before I do, I need to really, really thank you for your pioneering career and celebrate you for all you achieved.

Lots of love

Gemma
Xx

Chapter Threads

The League of Coloured Peoples (LCP) – British Civil Rights Organisation dedicated to campaigning against racial discrimination, founded in 1931.

Pan-Africanist – an advocate for the ideology of Pan-Africanism, which promotes the solidarity, unity, and self-determination of all indigenous African people and the global African diaspora.

Dr Imaobong Umoren – Associate Professor in the Department of International History at The London School of Economics and Political Science.

Cast Broadly – the world broadcast comes from the idea of 'casting broadly'. Could it originally have pertained to spells?

****A young woman*** – maybe Gemma, maybe not. A style of literary dissociation inspired by modern Danish writer Olga Ravn's book, *My Work*.

George Orwell – the pen name of Eric Arthur Blair, who was an English poet / journalist / novelist and critic. *Animal Farm* and *1984* were among his most notable works.

masking – term for 'covering up' neurodivergence with coping behaviours, such as lambasting oneself for muddled timekeeping or feeling overwhelmed with everyday tasks but not knowing how to ask for guidance or support for fear of looking stupid.

RP – a posh, English way of speaking called 'the Queen's Speech' or Received Pronunciation.

Snake Beat PT II

Re-assssses
Re-affirm where you
re-side
Re-late
Relation
Re-asses
Re-affirm where
you re-side
Re-late

4

Audre Lorde

The brave world-building pioneer

'Caring for myself is not self-indulgence, it is self-preservation, and that is an act of political warfare.'

Audre Lorde from her 1988 collection *Burst of Light*

Born: 18 February 1934, Harlem, New York, United States
Died: 17 November 1992, Saint Croix, U.S. Virgin Islands
Star Sign: Aquarius
Pronouns: She / Her

It's hard to offer enough space in just a chapter for the legacy of Audre. Professor, philosopher, civil rights activist, intersectional feminist. Where to start with Audre Lorde? Where to end? Let's start with the poignant and cut-through complexity in how she described herself as a 'black, lesbian, feminist, socialist, mother, warrior, poet', which covers it pretty well and brings me to the point in question that there's no way to finish theorising the kinetic power of her and her work, now so deftly bound in veracious legacy. Between 1961 and 1968 she worked as a librarian in New York City. She went on to become a professor at City University of New York, and taught at Lehman College and John Jay College of Criminal Justice.

Her repertoire twirls the scholar in the most impactful of ways. Just when you think you've read a lot of her, there's more provocation and possibility to be found, thanks to the generosity in her style that acts as a kind of alchemy for the reader or listener.

She was born in the mid-1930s in Harlem, where the lands were originally called Quinnahung. The same lands that lie beneath the metropolis that we know today and where fertile muds were once chosen for growing food and tobacco, and led to the lush marshlands of the Wecksquaesgeek Indians / before the Dutch came and claimed it as theirs, naming the area in 1646 after a city in the Netherlands called Haarlem, followed by a period of English rule six years later when they tried to name it Lancaster //

Harlem was where Audrey Geraldine Lorde's parents came to when they arrived from the Caribbean. Her mother was born in Carriacou, one of the islands that make up what we know to be called The Grenadines, and her father in Barbados.

Her exceptional talent was obvious from a young age. She had such precision in her skill as a wordsmith that as a child she removed the 'y' from her name to give it more written artistic symmetry when she wrote it in full.

Audre Lorde

Audre Lorde

Audre Lorde
Lyrical & harmonic.

Her choice makes me think hard about the power of one's name. All of the Sisters' names I love to write down and say out loud. What's in the magic of the letters making up our names and how do we redefine what our parents' gave us, if we did /do not feel like it represents our truth somehow?

> 'If I didn't define myself for myself, I would be crunched into other people's fantasies for me and eaten alive.'
>
> Audre Lorde during a speech at Harvard University in 1982

Sister Synchronicity: nu wave humility vs assertiveness

The writers and thinkers whom we choose to open our hearts and minds to represent an ever interesting path of discovery, not just for the work they produce but for how they want their own identity and status to be perceived. I was really drawn to the writer bell hooks's decision to drop the capitalisation of her name on her book covers and then found out that many feminist writers of the 1970s were choosing to lose the capital at the time, in order to de-centralise themselves from their theory and work. It wasn't the writer who was important, more the message. It was a way of challenging conventional hierarchy and opening up humility as an invitation. Conversely, I've noticed that Audre's name often appears in all capitals on her book covers, even in her own 'biomythography'. She had spent time building a career in spaces where Black women were often ignored, especially queer ones. Was the symmetry and shape of her own name adaptation so early on in her life a prophecy and exercise in having to learn resilience and pride in her very own written word, in preparation for the knockbacks she would go on to face? Like spells and wishes of enduring wisdom, does a capitalised printed name remind us to recognise the importance of the person behind the words, that might even be able to enhance and change our lives?

I like my name – the Gemma bit makes me smile, its ripple of precious gems and visual suggestiveness of mermaids' tails. I like how it's claimed in Italian with melodrama, bounces in beams of market-trading-harkening-grit in places where pies are served, and contains the double mm's for lingering hums when said . . . I've found lots of camaraderie in the G, when I come across other Gemmas whose parents chose the G over the J (so many of us, born in the 1980s or 1990s). I like the Cairney bit too, how cairns translate as ancient Celtic burial grounds and how despite me not having a Scottish accent it plugs me into the ground when I am on Scottish soil. I'm content to evolve it, though. I'm happy to de-territorialise the notion of a name by dropping the capitals, mark my flag as one made of silk that changes in harmony with the weather. I want my thoughts to be everlasting and not set, in service and full of incompleteness as the journey continues. That's what I'd like my name to mean.

gemma cairney 

great lengths and great loops, in fanciful play whilst forming my own handwriting

i remember practicing my signature for hours

when I

was young.

What about yours? when you say it aloud does it make you feel good?

Do you ever get to play with the way you write it down these days?

Growth, Heat 'n' Healing

Audre documented a complicated relationship with her parents, one where discipline and worry-for-her convoluted the unconditional parental love so many of us need to feel when we are children. She graduated from high school in 1951, and not long after, a huge row saw her packing her bags and leaving home for good. Independence came at an early age, as did a search for nurture and self-love. It is a wonder, upon reflection, that she was able to love as much as she did in her life with the grief and complexity that ensued as she became an adult.

It's moving to think that she still lived, loved, moved and honoured the absoluteness of friendship and relationships throughout her life, despite wounds and punitive parts of her past. Undeterred by a hard past, Audre spent one year in 1954 studying at National Autonomous University in Mexico. It's there that she affirms the impact on her of embracing both agency and her sexuality, while watching the arts scene thrive in underground spoken word gigs and the strength of unity in bars and hangouts where same-sex relationships were of no consequence or taboo, and radical politics were discussed in the heat of a vibrant Cuernavaca . . . around an hour and a half outside of Mexico City, filled with cobbled streets and surrounded by hills.

Over the years, she had many friends and lovers, and wrote of long, hot afternoons spent sipping brandy with her girlfriends in their underwear when they were still young women.

In one of her most notable works, *Zami: A New Spelling of My Name*, published in 1982, Audre reframes form entirely by inventing a bold blend of memoir, myth, history and biography in what she coins 'biomythography'. In this new form she focuses on her own life and includes stories of growing up and tending to an identity of contrasting textures and aural geography from having parents who were immigrants from the Caribbean in 1930s Harlem. Bit by bit, she deepens an understanding of herself as a woman with flaws, formidability and a core solidarity shared with the women around her, both in friendship and in romantic love, always embracing the parts of herself that are proudly lesbian.

When Audre was 16 her best friend Genevieve died by suicide. Audre's grief seared through her writing style and work for the rest of her life. In *Zami*, she lists the things they never got to do together, including writing a book. It prompts me to write lists of what I never got to do with my friend Caroline. When writing the list of things we never did, I realise that we actually got to do quite a lot: we were two friends lucky enough to spend a lot of time trying to live our dreams, going to awards ceremonies together, taking trips, shopping together . . . If I have ever loved you, I will likely have spent time trying on clothes with you. One of the things we didn't get to do, though, was watch one another have healthy romantic relationships at the same time as one another, or spend time on the beach with my daughter. I would have loved for Caroline to meet my daughter. I can only imagine her laughing at **Rita's** whimsical and giggling routines now.

Immortal effect

The network of great writers spawned by Audre's legacy is undoubtedly never ending. In Alexis Pauline Gumbs's epic non-linear biography of Audre – *Survival is a Promise* – Alexis exquisitely offers deep ode to the many dimensions of Lorde by intertwining geological, earthly and political references inspired by access to thorough study and rare archives but at the same time creates new and refreshed theory and theology by rejecting chronology in the format and using Audre's epic quotes to start chapters that lead you in unexpected directions, cementing her immortality and purposeful inspiring nature.

My friend Tia has an ode to Audre tattooed on their skin. Tia moved to the island of Jamaica to build a home and eat fruit grown from the land where coincidentally our individual great-grandparents were born within a few hours' drive of each other, and whose grandparents were likely born across the seas.

I speak to Tia on video call and we connect over our admiration and love for Audre Lorde:

> I love Audre so much, I've got Zami tattoos on me. Being able to separate a love of women from sexuality and being able to understand friendship more deeply . . . I think that's how Audre's really supported me in her work. Because as a queer person, I'm like, yeah, I love women. I'm attracted to women and I always want to be around women. But then there's being able to live like that, specifically the book *Zami*, I could identify in a more expansive light and also understand that reflection of how I love myself and in a separated way from sexuality, I actually really struggled to love myself and really struggled to love women. I know that her work has helped me to create that separation as a queer person. I really appreciate and value that. I also must say all of the references hit so much harder now that I actually live in the Caribbean, because . . . I see womanhood and sisterhood here, and then read back through some of the things that she was saying and it makes even more sense. Like the magnitude of it, becomes vast.
>
> Tia, artist, world builder and DJ, on how sister Audre has left an effect on them.

I'm struck by how a simple act such as writing can hold such gravitational power, for both writer and reader. Audre's pantheon is one of arresting essay, education / activism and mytho-poetry (the latter being a genre-defying style that invokes spirituality). Like Pamela Colman Smith, Audre is another woman (albeit from a different time) who confused others in her refusal to express herself typically or be easily defined.

She went on to live a life full of thinking, disrupting convention by communicating ideas and putting herself in the heart of positive action, unapologetically focusing her storytelling gifts not only on herself – but on others. She worked to rehabilitate convicts by facilitating a practice on using the power of one's voice and story to practice social justice. A moment to consider how important this work is, when still today 37 per cent of people in prison in the USA are Black when only 13 per cent of the population are Black.

She also publicly stood up for herself whenever she found a glass ceiling for Black women, whether in publishing, civil rights or academia, and continued to live a life of truth and of fighting for both bliss and equality.

In 1980, Audre co-founded (with **Barbara Smith** and **Cherríe Moraga**) Kitchen Table: Women of Color Press, the first US publisher solely dedicated to publishing women of colour. Its name symbolised the heart of connection and sustenance in any home.

Audre was inspired by West African spirituality, which had started to cross over to the United States through aural folklore and the diaspora. Isn't it marvellous how stories land upon us when we need them most? Especially those of us who have been displaced for generations and whose ancestors held strong through the confinements of being deemed 'lesser' by society. Some connections are in our inherited consciences regardless of oppression. Audre references 'Afrekete' or 'Eshu' in *Zami* and her earlier work *The Black Unicorn*. These are two names for the same messenger of the Orisha-Vodu gods and humans. Their role as accomplished linguists and orators is to translate the different languages between the two worlds. I feel a deep connection in my tapestry of Sisterhood with that same combination of lore and storytelling, via the divine, via goddess and myth. I've spent time seeking the mystics and witches, current and present, in order to be understood. If we are to go beyond the fear of appropriation and celebrate our shared identification as women / and our potential, we can work better together in overcoming some of the hardest challenges we face.

Simply put,

we

are

better

together.

Uses of the Erotic: The Erotic as Power, a poet's response

One of Audre's most profound and cited works is her essay called 'Uses of The Erotic'. In it she delivers a defiant and fresh reclamation of enjoyment and pleasure for women everywhere, beyond misogyny and realms away from the lens of pornified titillation. She describes the erotic as the 'opposite of the pornographic'. The essay is DEEP. You can hear her reading it on YouTube and it's best listened to spoken in her words of warm and unwavering truth, humour, and welcome to a better way to live out our many gifts. She spans criticism of objectifying women as only being allowed to contextualise eroticism in the bedroom and invites the undeniable oppression as a result of commodification and greed.

> The principal sorrow of any system which defines the good in terms of profit rather than in terms of human need, or which defines human need to the exclusion of the psychic and emotional components of that need – the principal horror of such a system that it robs our work of its erotic value, its erotic power and life appeal and fulfilment.[1]

In it, Audre argues that embracing wholeheartedness, embodied intensity, and excitement beyond sexual eroticism but in our every day lives, will release us from patriarchal suppression and squashing down of big feelings, including happiness.

For any of us, yearning for a language to explain our life's search for richness and an unabashed sensuality that merges through and softens the brutalism and exhaustion we can face in the expectation of being so many 'aspirational' versions . . . like sleep deprived mothers / working womxn in thankless jobs / sexy lovers / beautiful fair maidens etc . . . 'Uses of the Erotic' invites us to remember a powerful emotion available to us at most points – an ecstatic wonder of sorts that can been seen in the fruits and nature of a life that is loved and refuses self sabotage, or flagellation.

I sent the full essay to my friend, the writer Hollie McNish, when we were talking about the sensation of the act of writing and she responded with this:

> Reading Audre Lorde's 'Uses of the Erotic' was like acknowledging a heartbeat that I have been hearing and feeling and ignoring for years, for fear it was a silly thing I ought to be ashamed of or silence. In terms of my love of poetry, which,

until now, and strange now I think of it, I have never admitted to really loving, really enjoying but always dismissed it, almost embarrassed of how, well, erotic, it feels to me to sit in silence at a desk with a pad of paper and pen and work out how the feeling and thoughts within my body might pattern the page in the way I deem most exciting or comfortable. The idea of not being embarrassed by the excitement, the joy, the something unnameable which I feel exploding from my insides when laughing with friends or sidling up to my lover or watching beloveds eat a large and ripe piece of fruit, is here, and it's no longer something I will ever describe as ridiculous, or hysterical, or chaotic. The idea of the 'erotic guide' within me is now fermented in my mind and this idea has changed everything for me. The erotic is not only found in the bedroom. No, it never has been. Don't believe the lies!

I saw a surrealist piece of theatre created and performed by two performance artists (Julia Malsi and Paulina Lenoir) with clowning technique, in which they dressed as nuns and ended up in their birthday suits, navigating themes of friendship and mental health, all staged in a former gents' locker room during Edinburgh Fringe Festival, and all with the score of Audre's voice reciting 'Uses of the Erotic' interspersed in sections throughout. It made for powerful and freeing work.

Performance & Poetry? Are they the last bastions of evoking enlightened transformation in the palpable drudgery of feeling helpless?

Audre loved to dance.

My tears roll when watching the only film made about her life. It's called *The Berlin Years 1984–1992*, in which her presence and spirit is portrayed as one of unapologetic seeking and liberation. I know all of us who ache to dance together have this constructive possibility inside. I have decided I would like to dance every morning in my kitchen. In *The Berlin Years 1984–1992* Audre's peers and students and friends talk about her with such gratitude. Not only did she challenge them intellectually and emotionally but it's as though she summoned their capacity for joy as a balm for their pain. She would dance vigorously with words in poetry and with her body at celebrations.

For those of us
Who are imprinted with fear
Like a faint line in the centre of our foreheads

An extract of A Litany For Survival by Audre Lorde published in 1978 as part of the collection, *The Black Unicorn*.

Audre is everything. She is fables disguised as poems; poems disguised as essays.

She left a published portfolio of poetry collections, essays and documented speeches. Her words can change things. They are brave, confident, and they challenge. Why is it still so exciting for a woman's legacy to be written down with such confidence? Audre wrote about love, race, childhood trauma, spirituality and living as a Black lesbian mother and academic with vigour and a total lack of apology. She's an elder stewarding and inspiring so many other thinkers and writers to write their way through the possible transmutation of trauma into something more powerful.

In 'A Litany For Survival', a poem Audre wrote in 1978 as part of her *Black Unicorn* collection, she writes about self-worth and the value in the lives of anyone who has been neglected. It makes for a heartbreaking ode to the unsung.

For those of us who live at the shoreline
standing upon the constant edges of decision
crucial and alone.

There's a rousing feeling to Audre's published work. It galvanises and brings people together and offers the tantalising possibility that we might revive mythology as part of our everyday lives, inspiring us to write our own stories and to not be afraid to face up to the inner, outer and underworlds of our experience. I wonder what she would have made of this messy world today?

I think it's how I became drawn to the woo woo in my adult life. I needed a sort of somatic knowing and non-logical wonder to anchor me in contrast to the world around me, where we're so often engrossed in our phones and encouraged to be wrapped up in other people's business or curating ours to perfectionism and thankless productivity.

I felt like I had to take an upcycling approach to reinventing how I lived in my mid-thirties. How could I, having worked in showbusiness during my rookie twenties, take my craft which had become communication and solidarity into an adulthood that could be safer for my mental health? I looked at the sea and wondered. I learned how to read my tarot cards and got into breath of fire in Kundalini yoga. I read poems written by Black women who were survivors and did my best to forgive everything that's ever harmed me (myself included). I made a vow that I would scoop up all that has been wonderful, and focus on all that I've been gifted and lucky enough to learn, and always remember the awe I had as a little me, and remember that I still had such capacity for joy and for new beginnings. I didn't realise it at the time, but I was creating space by roaring all my regret into crashing waves: making space for my daughter, by remembering all that I think is beautiful and how much I am in love with living.

[BREATH/EXHALE]

It's scientifically proven that our brains problem-solve more efficiently when we dance in groups of people.[2]

Lorde's deep belief in communities coming together to shape policy and culture is a palpable thread of her legacy and one that crackles me forward. I wonder if bravery had to be at the centre of her choices, working in groups of vulnerable and marginalised people, teaching in institutions before she'd even had much experience.

For the last eight years of her life (1984–1992) Audre spent most of her working years in Berlin as a visiting professor at the Free University, inspiring her students to embrace their inner identities, write their thoughts down and express their own stories. Her work left a huge imprint on the Black diaspora and the intersecting feminist movements of Germany healing and reintegrating from fascism and war.

She wanted to find community and advocacy with other women who felt the same.

> It is that very difference which I wish to affirm, because I have lived it, and survived it, and wish to share that strength with other women.
>
> Audre Lorde, *The Cancer Journals*, 1980.

I think about my face and its contradictory frown lines. I read Audre's words like she's a psychic massaging my soul here in the future. How did she do it? I would so love to talk to her. I am excited by how one person can leave a body of work that inspires such different forms of expression. Like how Lorde's poetry rippled out to Tia who essentially creates mytho-movement-in motion on dance floors and lays physical path for moving through the world differently by self building a sanctuary for themselves and their community. Perhaps we would not have discovered the breadth of our abilities if it hadn't been for Audre, on whose energetic shoulders we stand.

I invite us to STAND TO ATTENTION and invite AUDRE's legacy to live within our bookshelves and for her words to fill our atmospheres on days we feel overwhelmed and lacking a unique philosophy on living far away from the patriarchy. If I'm introducing you to the work of Audre for the first time, then it's my utter pleasure to expand the Sisterhood and quality of complex insight into Black Feminism and Queerness laced with emotional precision that's in her writings. If you are seasoned with her ingredients and tools already, then none of this will come as a surprise, I suspect. Except for perhaps a final thought around being in devotion to an artist's work that not only invites reverence but also their humanness and fallibilities. There's a sense overall in the body of work over the decades that Audre worked tirelessly, that she was always open, always learning, always growing without imposing constructs of perfectionism that has us doing everything we can to keep the mess out of a life, that when lived wholly, always occurs.

End of May 2020

A wonderful open-ended stay in the white cliffs of Thanet

Dear Audre

What a mess it all is.

Your words speak to my mourning today.

We are on lockdown, a new term that makes us all shudder and feel controlled by politicians. I couldn't bear to watch the news since this first happened a few months ago, but that choice has today become an act of preservation and survival, as I've been alone for months now and this means a lot of thinking time and going to bed and waking up and cooking alone. I needed this, but, like I said, I have a lot of time with the evolving courage and vulnerability of my unshared thoughts and something truly sickening has happened in the world and now a feeling oozes from the core of our existence like pus. A young man was publicly murdered by the police in Minneapolis. He'd been stopped by the police for allegedly using a counterfeit $20 bill in a convenience store, and an officer held him down until he could no longer breathe. It was filmed and has been seen the planet over. It's baked into the nerve of the masses, and collective thoughts have now turned to the lives of Black people. A movement has erupted. Folk are putting posters in their windows saying 'Black Lives Matter'. There's something about everyone watching this murder on screens and the time we have to breathe in what we see, now that we're all locked down, that has catapulted honesty and sparked a moral obligation to unpick every part of our lives that is linked to racism and stand up, demand accountability, and make change.

I didn't watch the footage of George Floyd being killed. I couldn't traumatise myself in such a way.

I'm galvanised, shaken and having some of the most affirmative conversations about race in my life. Though I have to admit it feels in conflict to visions I was already having that the world may actually be ending. It's why I've found myself in this temporary, rented home that's been constructed by carving into a chalky cliff, right by the edge of the sea in a place called Ramsgate. I needed to be by the sea if the world is ending. Here was as good a sea as any, even if the town centre is a bit forgotten and decayed. From this house you can see the greens and blues of the ocean from all floors. The doors of my bedroom open out onto the changing tides. I've only managed to secure the house for a few months during this mad global pandemic, which I don't even know how to describe to you in the past, as it seems so sci-fi and modern. Ramsgate is in a place they call The Isle Of Thanet, made up of a cluster of three British seaside towns I know very well, called Margate, Ramsgate and Broadstairs. Here, it was once a literal isle that was separated by a channel off the coast of England. They say the name could come from a Celtic word – tan/teine – meaning 'bright' or 'fire' or it's from the Greek god Thanatos who was the personification of death. There are ancient burial grounds here that lie beneath us, but built over for hundreds of years. It's a historical English location, one that's seen Roman invasion, become the Victorian gentry's prime spot for **convalescing** and leisure, and most recently a cheaper alternative for folk outpriced by London to buy a much bigger house than they would have been able to afford in the city (which is a commutable distance). I like it here, even if it is The Isle of Death. Was being by water important to you? You wrote some of your most significant work while living on **Staten Island**. Pictures of the house where you lived make it look really special. I would love to see it one day. Water. There's so much of it in between myself and other humans that I feel connected to. It holds the memories that come to my dreams for no rhyme or reason, except for knowing that when I sleep close to water your writings ripple through my body, their grace and activation in every word. In my dreams your lines are spoken by folk I loved in past lives and in the future. Audre, I wish you were able to guide us on where to go from here . . . Because Black lives have always mattered and it's always been unequal and if everyone's ready to finally admit it (I had a text from an acquaintance earlier who apologised for their ignorance and asked what books they should read by Black authors on race) then we need your thoughts and clarity and stance. Some are suggesting everyone comes off Instagram for a day and shows solidarity with a 'black square' on their feed, another part of life that feels preposterous to try and explain to the past. We must be able to address the complicated functioning of anti Blackness and white supremacy in deeper, less corporate, and more heart-led ways. Do you think a revolution may be possible? One where the public are re-birthed into deep conscious reform and radical love?

We really need you right now. As you're not here, I will do my best to spread your works as far and as wide as I can, in the hope that it wasn't the end of the world I was foreseeing, but the end of what we knew.

Thank you for everything

Gemma
Xx

Snake Beat PT III

Re-late
Rationalise
Re-cog-nise
Open eyes

***

Audre Lorde

G – Sister Synchronocity

When I was growing up I was always told a story about how my name was meant to be Genevieve. 'I saw it on a name badge of an incredibly beautiful bunny in the playboy club in Park Lane and I knew I wanted to call my daughter that name, it felt so unusual,' was my mum's anecdote about it. Oddly enough, years later I became friends with the person in charge of artist liaison at Oxfam during the years I spent as an ambassador for the charity. Her name is Genevieve. We have been to Ethiopia together to meet women who are beekeepers and matriarchs, where we spotted an albino bee that was black and white. The sight of it made us ecstatic. Some real-life **glamour** magic from a bee.

Chapter Threads

nu – a new spelling of 'new' in ode to **Nubian**, sensibilities of which you'll notice in the rhythm of this book a few times. The Nubians are a significant ethno-linguistic group indigenous the the Nile Valley, encompassing northern Sudan and southern Egypt.

Rita – my daughter's shortened name.

Barbara Smith – feminist, socialist, writer, activist and scholar who is an important figure in the Black Feminist movement in the United States from the 1970s and currently.

Cherríe Moraga – theorist, playwright, poet, activist, professor and groundbreaker of Chicana (Xicanisma)[3] studies in the States from the 1970s and currently.

convalescing – gradually recovering health and strength after a serious illness, injury, or surgery, usually involving a period of rest.

Staten Island – an island borough of New York City accessible via bridge from Brooklyn and Manhattan via a famous free ferry.

glamour – originally a Scots word to describe a certain allure and magic through precious aesthetic, an allure through garments, adornment and style that has power to 'entrance'.

5

Jeanne Duval

Haitian; inspirational force of 1840s Paris demimonde; sex-working sorcerer

The Sister is already documented as a woman as powerful as Venus, but did you know that Venus is sometimes referred to as Earth's Sister?

Born: 1820 (month and exact place unknown)
Died: 20 December 1860
Star Sign: Unknown
Pronouns: She / Her

Jeanne Duval was the muse for some of the most acclaimed poetry of the nineteenth century – and yet because she has almost disappeared from view, much of what's known about her is based on speculation and guesswork.

She was the long-time lover of revered French poet Charles Baudelaire, who made her the subject of many of his poems. But since her death she's been largely forgotten. I have been compelled to glimpse amongst the shadows of her life and discover from traces this Sister who knew how to thrive and survive at the fluid edges of a society and theorise how it deserves reverence beyond Baudelaire's poetry – Jeanne was in Paris in the wake of the 1848 people's revolutions that swept through Europe – in the middle of radical change. Baudelaire is known to have pushed his heart and mind to the edges and judging by Jeanne's story he went crazy for her.

Some say she travelled to Europe as a child in the 1820s with her mother from Haiti, which had only been declared free from slavery after a revolution in 1804. Archival information about Jeanne often states that it's 'not known' whether she was born in Haiti or 'Santo Domingo', but the island wasn't bordered into two separate countries at this time (post revolution the Dominican Republic would emerge as a result of civil wars and more European invasion). This would mean Jeanne was born on the only whole island in the Caribbean free from forced slavery at the time. Some say it was Jeanne's Haitian-born grandmother on her mother's side, born in Guinea, who was sent to Nantes in France and forced to work as a sex worker and proves Jeanne was in fact born in France. Some say her mother was Black and her father was likely a white French man she had no contact with. We will never know.

It's not easy to decipher who Jeanne was but there has absolutely been something about her that has long compelled historians, art critics, biographers and scholars alike. Is it the ambiguity that reels folk in? The same undefinable 'strangeness' and 'untameable' vibrations that surrounded Pamela Colman Smith?

Let's imagine the nature and ambience of the island she travelled from. Haiti was quite multicultural, despite the French having been defeated in the uprising. The majority of the people were freed slaves of African descent and there were also doctors, priests, and other skilled workers who were French and had been granted citizenship, alongside some German and Polish soldiers who had fought on the side of the revolutionaries.

If she wasn't born there, did her mother tell her of the journey that had led to her being born?

Jeanne came of age in nineteenth-century Paris where she cultivated a life as an actress and cabaret performer and likely a **courtesan**. She belonged to the socially fluid '**demimonde**' – a world on the fringes of 'respectable society' – and held her own as easily among bohemians as among **debutantes**.

The shape shifts of Jeanne

It's debated that Jeanne may have met the wily French poet Charles Baudelaire when she was as young as 15, when he sent flowers to the theatre after seeing her perform. She ended up being his lover for over 20 years. Their relationship was tumultuous, not to mention violent. He once fractured her skull by throwing a vase at her.

Charles Baudelaire is still one of France's most revered and controversial poets. He didn't just write poetry about how beguiled he was by her and her celestial allure; he wrote about her incessantly to his mother. He refers to betrayal, infatuation and their many makeups and breakups in these letters. It's simply gutting that, upon his death in 1867, Baudelaire's mother is thought to have destroyed all the letters Jeanne had sent him. They could have offered us more clues into the incredible autonomy I imagine she had for much of their time together.

On a trip to Paris in 2023, I travelled to Rue Le Regrattier where she lived, to get a geographic sense of her life. I found the name of her street eerie as it means 'Street of the Headless Woman'. I walked along it, heart beating, feeling lucky enough to imagine Jeanne Duval walking down it every day in the 1840s. It was a location near to where Baudelaire resided at the Hotel Pimodan, also known as Hôtel de Lauzun, on the Île Saint-Louis, a previously glamorous residence for French noblemen that had fallen into disrepair after the revolution. It was here that Charles spent years smoking hashish and opium with friends and writing prolifically. But what was Jeanne doing while he was tripping? Did she continue to act and perform on stage, as she had in the Latin Quarter of the city when she was younger?

Baudelaire described her as the 'Venus Noire', his very own Black Venus. The planet Venus is dominated by volcanoes.

Les Fleurs du mal (The Flowers of Evil), originally published in 1857, includes many poems about Duval. In *Sed Non Satiata*, which translates as 'Insatiable Lust', Jeanne is fetishised as an exotic 'brown as night' lover who feels better to him than his beloved opium, but then quickly turns into an evil unsatisfiable character. 'Oh fearless demon! Pour a drink less hot!' he begs of his muse.

In '**La Chevelure**' he fashions an ode to her thick black hair:

Sweltering Africa and languorous Asia,
A whole far-away world, absent, almost defunct.

Baudelaire wasn't the only one fascinated by her. The renowned photographer **Nadar** famously shot her looking iconic in regal attire with a massive bow round her neck and flowers in her hair.

Manet famously painted her towards the end of her life, after she'd experienced a syphilis-induced stroke that left her apparently unable to feel or use the entire right side of her body. In his painting she wears a magnificent huge pale dress and seems to be reclining. A haunting image when you know about her life story and that she was so sick from a sexually transmitted disease.

She was otherwise virtually written out of a remarkable historic period, in a city buzzing with artistic innovation and political hope after yet another revolution. The survival of a young woman with dual heritage in a culturally eruptive European city in these times / any times is not something that can simply be brushed under the carpet. If Baudelaire's writing defied convention then so did Jeanne's existence.

In **Gustave Courbet**'s famous 1855 painting *The Painter's Studio: a real allegory summing up seven years of my artistic and moral life* it's said that Jeanne was scrubbed out of her place, where she had originally been painted standing next to Baudelaire, who is depicted with his head wistfully in a book in the right section of the epic, realist and gigantic picture which still hangs in the Musée d'Orsay in Paris. She was allegedly removed at Baudelaire's request. Courbet, likely aware of their stormy relationship, obliged. A ghostly silhouetted figure can just about be made out to this day, where she would have been. If she hadn't been erased, she would have been the only person with Black heritage in the picture.

Sister Synchronicity: It's not just me

Feeling particularly skint, hopeless and tired and walking with my big second-hand pram around the National Portrait Gallery of Scotland, one grey, mid-week afternoon I suddenly find myself facing a piercing stare from two photographs of a mixed race writer / visual artist / photographer with Scottish-Ghanaian heritage who I learn is the late Maud Sulter, who in these photographs is representing Jeanne Duval, in a permanent work called 'La Chevelure'. I'm confronted by the fact – when I see it written on a small plaque by the picture – that Duval had to sell her jewels and possibly her hair to survive at points. I draw in breath, for in this moment of feeling kinship with Duval I have the strongest sense that the terror that money can induce is a made-up idea designed to traumatise me and that it's actually moments of kismet and coincidence like this that may be what we should continue to strive for. I've been writing this book for years by this point, and in those years, I have moved countries and given birth and been left with no other option but to spend what savings I had, due to lack of funding and paid work opportunities. I've felt like I've always been working through a tense mix of excitement mixed with lack of self-worth that would sometimes take away the beauty of the writing process. And just when I need a sign to keep going, keep writing, and not look back, there it is: Sisters (Maud – the artist and Jeanne), staring at me and willing me to keep on. Commanding the importance of women's stories in a stare. Sulter says of the portraits that she developed a 'visual fascination' with Duval. In one of them, she wears a necklace of precious stone; in the other she holds a handful of cut hair in a bag.

> I'm very interested in the absence and presence in the way that particularly Black women's experience and Black women's contribution to culture is so often erased and marginalised. So it's important for me as an individual and obviously as a Black woman artist to put Black women back in the centre of the frame.
>
> Maud Sulter, on her photographic art

Infinite knots: for we are one and one of many and this is about our interconnections, our bloodlines, our powers, our thanks and our hairlines and I know that I must keep weaving, keep at this project and keep living a life with my eyes wide open and asking questions.

A Sense Memory: The wide world

I've done a lot of work on myself, dived headfirst into various kinds of therapy and support for nearly a decade. I've needed it. I didn't grow up in an adjusted environment; I didn't know how to stay healthy or nourish myself and put unnatural onus on a 'very 1990s understanding' that to 'be desired' by the opposite sex gave you the self-worth and needed attention to get by.

What a load of bullshit. I get a chance now to re-wire these notions (not something that everyone who grew up in such ways gets to do). I'm trying to build a beautiful, shame-free and reciprocal life for myself and others in a number of ways.

I know I sometimes live in what can be seen as a dream world, and I choose to do that, because sometimes it feels safer for me there. When you've been hurt, you have to restore some kind of order not to see the pain in everything. I've come to realise that there's an important and potentially enriching equilibrium to aspire to, one rooted in both the real world and an ethereal one, one that exists in the natural rhythm of my very own life. I need introspection but maybe I need outside help too. I'm vulnerable and neurodivergent and in order to let go of the othering of my own childhood I can, in the now, embrace how I'm different. Perhaps I'll spend a whole life finding some things trickier than others. I was never typical and it's sad that this was overlooked until now, but it's OK, in this season, these times, we will find societal empathy for divergently lived, complex lives.

A Sense Memory: Whirlwinds / from City to Town

We just kept on growing in our twenties, a bundle of beaming naivety, so close to one another, in a mixture of hotch-potch buildings where we kept up hope and optimism through mice-invasions, a burglary, health labyrinths, criminal landlords and rampant gentrification – just by living in the same neighbourhood. Out of a rabble of around 15 friends, none of us lived more than seven minutes' walk from one another, and that fact was beautiful enough to see us through quite a lot. We made sure each other got home safely at night, encouraged lightning-flash romances, and spontaneous parties, lent each other clothes and sat in the same Turkish café for hours and hours, talking out our insecurities and giggling with arms wrapped around one another, keeping each other warm, fed and safe. These were things that some of us didn't always get at home with our parents and caregivers, but those who knew how to provide them were generous with sharing these skills, and it was just lovely for those few years. I remember genuine delight being such a strong part of my twenties. Everyone's jobs in my gang were interesting too, and we talked about them in depth and with enthusiasm. But the fun we had was as important as our careers. I felt so lucky.

I was in love with my job and my friends.

It could be a dubstep rave where an artist would play the trombone, or an art opening where you were invited to look through cellophane at a vaginal-looking piece, or just feeling ecstatic at being given a free glass of supermarket wine. None of this was documented, of course. I wasn't so used to having a mobile phone as an appendage back then and would regularly lose my **Nokia 3310**. I hated phones (surprise surprise). Sometimes someone would bring out their digital camera and we'd pose in abstract and obviously inebriated ways, because the escapism and togetherness we sought weekend after weekend was already enough: we didn't crave the capturing of all in images, too. I thought this would last for ever, that we'd be able to one day afford the two-up, two downs we stomped past every day and keep being in the same 'hood. I imagined we'd cascade through our biggest moments in life together, be the 'tribe' people talk about being vital if / when we decided to have babies. But it wasn't true for us. I didn't know that history would have us scattered all over the UK and Europe. That we'd even lose one of our gang to cancer. That our chosen careers would create a huge spectrum of incomes and that some of us would need to prioritise their actual families being nearby when they had children. But, oh, those children would be the sweetest to hang with, looking like a squish of your most favourite faces in the world. I didn't know that it would be hard work but also so special and a luxury to head to a different country to see an old friend. That to grow is to expand and nurture parts of yourself and that going to the coolest party might not thrill me as much as it did at a different part of my life. I loved those days and I still love those people and I thank them every time I see them for going on the ride with me.

A Sense Memory: Redirection. Signs. Sisterhood everywhere

Flowers of Good and Evil is the name of a concept-based art piece by the late African American contemporary artist Lorraine O' Grady. It's an ongoing project that started in 1998 and continues, open ended . . . in the way some of the most compelling stories do. It consists of a series of photoshopped and layered photographs of Baudelaire and Jeanne, as a way of remarking on the artist's fascination with them both. In her essay 'Study of Flowers of Good and Evil' she explains in more detail how her fascination became so drawn out partly because she just couldn't find enough material on Jeanne Duval so she almost had to keep going to keep the progress and eternality of her alive. O' Grady hints at forgotten stories not being able to have an end.

We see you, Jeanne.

A Sense Memory: Elders

An eccentric elder in a raspberry-coloured beret walks into a juice franchise in central London. She walks slowly, the colours of her garments are felt, vibrant. Despite her gentle pace, she is dynamic. I notice that she has kind and smiling eyes and that she seems to luxuriate unfolding in the time taken to choose her smoothie order, reminding me that moments of choice should be celebrated in our abundant lives. She has no device attached to her person, which is physically obvious as everyone else in the establishment is connected to a smart phone, lit-up by Apple emblems cyber-phying the collective body, cords upon cords . . . charging. Entanglements // memories // batteries // MINDS FULL, despite them all being decades younger than the elder lady in the raspberry beret.

I wonder, as I often do in these reckonings about our contemporary age . . . why we don't all just run away and tend the land together, be gentle and safe, wear raspberry berets and play music that makes our eyes smile. Thoughts begin to churn, thoughts of resistance to the isolation and rapidness of modern times come quickly. How can I help save us all from this aching epidemic of loneliness? I never knew it would become so radical to want to connect so badly, to want to talk, to want everything to be slower and lighthearted, grounded in earth and without such exhaustion from our reliance on a digital world. If my life had gone a different direction, if I had not created a repertoire of live broadcast and choosing to experience and explore the electricity of live music and dancing in groups, what would I be believing in? Would I even notice how lonely the encouragement of 'singular' experience was making me? But if I see it, what do I do? If I see how addicted we all are to our devices and how sad it is making us, then what can I do? I can write urgently about the power of connections, the love found in unity, and whisper a wish that the old lady in the raspberry beret staring quietly into space, and noticing the world, can teach us all something. Even though she is old enough to have lived through a world war and fragments of all the others we're now facing, does her serenity give her resilience and vitality? Generations of people listening to pre-recorded and edited conversations, planning our next interaction on a screen could learn from her and slow down.

I don't know anything. But I know what makes me feel good.

Love conversation,
Love affection
Love intimacy,
Love people,
Love laughter,
Love looking into eyes,

March 2024

Dear Jeanne

I'm writing from one of my favourite places on earth. I'm tempted to not even disclose where, it's that precious.

Yet I've decided I must tell you where it is. It's an ole fisherman's cabin, painted a near shade of cobalt blue in a sacred and unexpected cove on the East Coast of Scotland. My love and I have stayed here for our birthdays (which land within four days of one another) every year, for the past three. I am now pregnant with my first child which feels quite different to the newness of our romance when we first came to eat freshly caught crab and drink whisky and wine. Then I felt giddy, raucous and despite no inklings of what was to come, swept and whisked in the moment and sensation of beauty. Now I feel the grounding of physical gestation and of making space as I time travel into ideas of future life.

It's here, in this very place, within red rocky crags and a sea crashing full of ghosts that a named 'forefather' of Geology called James Hutton, was once able to understand that the world was in fact so much older than everyone had originally thought at the time, (this was around 1788, 32 years before you were born, well they suspect you were born anyway – when were you born by the way?) due to the sandstone rock formation possessing something he described as 'angular unconformity'. How wild to think that 'deep time' was being proved before we walked this planet. The sandstone's layers and jaggedyness here is said to cover an unimagined 60–80 million years. It's called Siccar Point and it's breathtaking, to look at, even more profound to breathe and sleep in among, the sandstone is an unusual red colouring because of iron oxide and there is no place I'd rather write than with the fire on than the Blue Cabin, listening to radio and imagine the unimaginable.

I am drawn to the description of 'angular unconformity' that somehow defying scientific history is possible. I wonder how many of us, all these years later in the 21st century could thrive and find belonging in a cosmology called 'angular unconformity'?

In the deep, time travel and blur between real life and dreaming here I envisaged you and wondered what the experience of your love might be with Baudelaire . . .

The pleasure of watching him leave was as pleasurable as watching him orgasm. Jeanne Duval thought to herself as the door slammed shut and her lover would start his hurried scamper down the stairs, she wondered why he moved so quickly, was it a symptom of his furiousness? Was it inside of him, molten bubbling, and did it hurt? He was in despair about lots . . . other people, other men, especially other men that wrote. Jeanne would smile and nod and busy herself with menial acts of distraction. She would listen, yes but move, and do things like open the shutters to let the light pierce the gloom of what had been a long night of sex and talking. Or pour a drink really slowly into a pair of ornate **Pokal glasses**, pleased at the blood-like liveness of Claret in beautiful glassware, and drift between the veils of her memories and drunken imaginings . . . Here she remembered how birds spoke to her as a child when she was in Haiti and escape was all around her, in birdsong, in the whispers from the mouths of elders, in the smell of the soil after rain. Escape and its unfolding potential tranquility, a mind state of zoning out it was always so available to her and it's when he was gone she'd sing to herself, dance with her belly in the mirror, love herself and her things with pride and far away from the rage spell he tried to conduct with venemous pondering. She loved herself and her things in a self possessed paradise that Charles would absurdly try to grasp at, but couldn't because it was inside of her and not a material that could be inhabited, or taken.

I wish for the child inside my womb right now to have the potential for the imagination to nurture them as much as everything in the outside world. **I at the same time, hope they never have to conjure it only to combat bad energy inflicted or projected upon them.**

Thank you for the survival, Jeanne, to write about you was a privilege. Despite the attempted erasure of your importance and existence I'm so grateful that you have compelled great scholars to honour your abstract legacy. I know you to be more than a 'muse' but an example of radical love. I can only hope that in your relations, pleasure and mystery was reciprocated and that you enjoyed splendour. Like James Hutton's geological discoveries, I hope somewhere in the other worlds of deep time's past, you are gratified to know that beautiful memories of you will be uncovered . . . Photographs of you in a dress that looks like it's printed with the shapes of seaweed on the skirt and majestically holding a riding crop . . . will surface from archives and repaint a picture of dignity . . . beyond your end being reported as just one of ill-health and poverty. Nothing can take away from the strength in your facial expression of these photographs and leads me further to posthumously hope that there was as much respect for you in your life as there was extraction.

Snake Beat PT IV

Trans-gress,
Trans-cribe,
Trans-late,
Trans-ition
Trans-gress,
Trans-cribe.

Jeanne Duval / Grace Jones

A Sense Memory: New York City, 2022

Three generations of Black women, holding court, arm in arm, sauntering past and delighting me with their cadence and hairstyles: all gorgeous, all chattering magic. I am heading towards the gallery that they are just leaving. Blackness, joy, irreverence, ingenuity. I feel it everywhere, and it makes my legs spring and the backpack on my back feel like it's complete with a jet that can make me fly. They are the best-dressed family I've ever seen, different stories beaming from their faces. The eldest gestures towards me, 'Honey, you look fantastic,' she says with lips painted in blue lipstick.

'Oh, thank you so much, that's such a compliment coming from you – you are all the most amazingly dressed peeps in the universe . . .' I reply. We giggle and beam some more, through our eyes, through our coos, in harmony, and I head into the gallery to be submerged.

NYC, where the concrete speaks

I've always felt home in New York. Perhaps it was my mother who passed an awe for the place onto me. She lived on the East Coast of America with her family in the 1970s and went to school in Manhattan, where she wore bell bottoms, styled her hair with the same golden-tonged flicks sported by **Farah Fawcett**, and would tell my sister and I tales of both glamour and danger submerged with reckless teen fun and romance and the high buildings and the high stakes of this glamorous city. Or maybe it was the 'indie sleaze' developed later which I can sometimes associate with New York the family tree of rock 'n' roll, which rolled over from The Velvet Underground, then Ramones into The Strokes and landed in my London circles, where we felt lit up by wearing second-hand leather jackets two sizes too small for us and smoked the same cigarettes. Or was it the world of pre-gentrified Brooklyn, where Blackness 'n' renaissance resonated through paintings, jazz, progress, 1970s-Black-feminism-into-the 1980s, 1990s . . . swirling in the wind . . . Spike Lee's *She's Gotta Have It*. The sounds and visuals of this era of artistry speak to me so deeply. Then of course there's the **queens of voguing** from that era, and omg, the queens of hip-hop, who made so much of their work in New York: **Faith Evans**, **Lil Kim**, **Monie Love**, **Mary J. Blige** to name but a few, and RnB – SWV, a femme trio of power and strength. Three women, holding court, delighting me with rap, new jack swing, hip hop and soul wrapped in cross-Atlantic references from the United States to the United Kingdom where I was listening from, helping me from a formative age carve out a sensuous understanding of what the word united truly means. I felt it was the music that UNITED us to what was called the United States. Sentient diasporic, understandings, planting my two feet on the ground, rousing my own urges to hold court myself.

Now it's 2022, and the exhibition I'm going to is a retrospective of the notorious force that was **Jean-Michel Basquiat**. It's called 'King Pleasure', and it already feels different to what I've seen of his work before. It has been put together by his sisters. I can feel the familial connection as soon as I enter. Siblings quite literally unpacking their experience of their globally renowned, everlastingly copied, gifted, troubled, late brother, and all done with loving grace, generosity and posthumous healing.

I feel like the pieces that I see are literally moving and jumping out of the canvases. Like I can somehow hear the rage-filled scrawls and repetitions in his signature crown drawings and open-mouthed dinosaurs, complete with jagged teeth calling out the injustices of the art-world / the disparity culture all around him. They are transporting me as though pictures-are-portals to a vibrant and loud Chelsea, New York, in the 1970s. I feel the past conversations stirring inside of me, even though I wasn't born then and this building that I'm in, the Starett-Leigh, takes on new weight. Right in this very moment, it's a sleek gallery space. During the 1970s it would have been just another warehouse, vast architecture for the hard, fast industrialism of the times. At one point, this building was the world's largest industrial freight warehouse made especially to reduce freight congestion in the 1930s as the city became a hub of the railroads – the very same railroads our sister Pamela Colman Smith's family worked to create – criss-crossing booming North America / Turtle Island.[1]

Links, lines,
networks and trade.

What would Basquiat have thought of his sisters tending with such grace to his legacy, not just hanging his paintings but recreating his studio, complete with materials and exhibiting never-seen-before sketch books?

I walk around the space that recreates his studio, which had been on the famous Great Jones St from 1983 to 1988. There are art books, an old boxy TV turned on, and huge canvases – all in motion. I let tears fall as I watch videos of his sisters describing how special it has been to curate this experience. I start to think about how we are all children once in our lives and how play and imagination never leave us. I think about Basquiat's comrades, his associates and all he bounced off in his seeking-of-freedom against a supremely harsh landscape for a curious, questioning Black man.

I think of the art parties Basquiat went to and how magical and serendipitous it was that so many conceptual and expansive thinkers came together in this same area. I think about whether those 'seekers' were drawn to those parties by invisible cosmic magnets. I think about whether some holy gut-led cartography guided them all to the same place. I think about . . . Grace Jones.

And in that very moment, I look up to see two words etched in repeat on a page of one of the sketchbooks on display.

Great Jones
Great Jones
Great Jones
Great Jones
Great Jones
Great Jones

There it is on repeat in Basquiat's signature handwriting, and for the blink of an eye I transmute the word Great into Grace. I didn't know whether to laugh, whether I was just being ludicrous by connecting the dots. But did they hang out? Was Grace ever on Great Jones St? Did Jean Michel ever become intoxicated by the brilliance of Grace Jones, like I had been lucky enough to once in her presence? I started imagining it.

Great Grace Jones, in the scene, of an eve, on Great Jones.

The great,
the AMAZING,
all the grace,

in style

in frequency

in vogue.

Sister.

Great

Grace

Jones.

Chapter Threads

Nadar – Gaspard-Félix Tournachon, known as Nadar, or Félix Nadar, was a French photographer, caricaturist, journalist, novelist and balloonist.

Manet – Édouard Manet, a 19th-century French modernist painter and contemporary of Jeanne Duval's.

Gustave Courbet – French painter who ironically (in his decision to erase Jeanne Duval in his monumental painting *The Painter's Studio: a real allegory summing up seven years of my artistic and moral life*) led the Realist movement in which artists committed to only painting what they could see.

courtesan – an old term for a sex worker or mistress who provided a service exclusively for the wealthy.

demimonde – a collective living on the fringes of obedient societal norms.

debutantes – a young woman who is formally introduced to 'high society'.

La Chevelure – translates into English as 'The Hair' and is a famous poem of Charles Baudelaire in the 'Spleen and Ideal' section of a collection called *Flowers of Evil* from 1861.

Nokia 3310 – a popular mobile phone in the early noughties also now known as a 'burner'.

'hood – another 'hood of great importance.

Pokal glasses – a goblet originating from the 17th century for the use of drinking toasts.

Farah Fawcett – born in 1947, Farah Fawcett is an actor who was most famously an original Charlie's Angel and wore her hair with signature flicks.

queens of vogueing – vogueing is an iconic dance, full of fashion posing to have come out of the underground Harlem drag and ballroom scene originating as early as the 1960s.

Lil Kim – uniquely fierce rapper from the United States, who was huge in the mid-90s.

Monie Love – English-born hip-hop artist who emigrated to the United States in the late 80s and became a successful rapper and radio personality.

Mary J Blige – Hip-Hop and Soul artist born in the Bronx of NYC in 1971 and went on to be one of the top selling artists of the scene.

Jean-Michel Basquiat – born in 1960, Jean Michel Basquiat was hugely prominent artist of the Neo-expressionism movement, rising to fame in the 1980s.

6

Grace Jones

The living hula-hooping Afrofuturist legend

'The future is no sex . . . I have just as much woman in me as I have man. It's just a matter of channelling the energy into which way you use it.'

Grace Jones in *Interview* Magazine, 1984

Born: 19 May 1948, Spanish Town, Jamaica
Sign: Taurus,
Pronouns: She / Her

Long before I met this goddess, I had admired the legendary Jones. Born in Spanish Town, Grace Jones was one of seven kids. She moved to the United States aged 13, to Salina, a northern suburb of Syracuse, New York. During her college years she was persuaded by a drama tutor to go on a trip with him to Philadelphia. She didn't come back, and instead took part in acid trials, and experienced hippie culture.

This Sistxr epitomises what it means to be a force of nature. This is, after all, the woman who, when I asked her what she'd do if she saw a shark while enjoying her beloved hobby, sea swimming, replied simply, 'Why! I'd punch him in the nose.'

I met Grace on the river in the Chelsea part of London and she was predictably and un-disappointingly formidable, but not scary in the way she's often depicted. We met when her memoir had just been published, and she'd said yes to me recording an interview with her over dinner in a restaurant of her choice. I was in ecstasy; Grace had only said yes to two interviews, and I was one of them.

'I want you to know, I'm not here to make you into a caricature', I said to her from the start of our conversation. 'I want to create an archive, documenting what a feminist icon you are.' We met eye to eye in that moment . . . warmth, a study of magnificence on my part, integrity pouring between us and into our exchange. To this day, it's the most memorable interview I've ever done, for the fact that it felt like an out-of-body experience. Once we'd finished, I remember saying to my producer, 'I have no idea if I did a good job there, but I do know that experience changed my life'.

I've always found that there is a certain authenticity that hangs in the air in the company of living legends who were around and making art in the 1970s; the partiers and the artisans of their craft from back then were born at a time of huge postwar change, when being an artist meant melding allure with grit and innovation. It was a time in the United States when the Civil Rights movement had cemented itself into the cultural historic landscape for well over a decade and the Stonewall Riots were feeding a ferocity into disco, house music and simultaneously hip-hop was being invented from street culture, all out of needs for something new and perhaps ancestral callings for our hearts to beat in unison in big crowds, for our muscles and joints to stretch and move together to beats? If you wanted to be part of an exciting future you got futuristic, especially if you were marginalised. Movement and art were of high importance and a portal to express yourself and perhaps alchemise oppressive force into fun, into money, into travel. Those that made enough to 'go places' did, both the curious and the ritzy not only lived internationally but hung out together, danced together, went along to one another's photoshoots, shows, exhibitions and gigs wherever they were, in a mish mash of high / low surroundings. Independent magazines celebrated and platformed subculture. Art and culture as an organism had its key figues informing one another and interchanging forms were encouraged. It gave those artists a unique quality. Those that survived the drugs and soul searching of the 1960s came out with a 'don't give a fuck' attitude that I find so very unique. There's a sense of sophistication to the era-specific opulence about them that I think many of us making art now would never be able to experience without feeling guilty. Climate change wasn't mentioned back then for example. It wasn't in any zeitgeist to talk of the hardship of survival. Instead, a 'jet-set', living for the moment, 'mile-high', crystal champagne flute clinking lifestyle was glamourised with an ambience that isn't existent now beyond cosplay by some billionaires. Imagine what fashionable folk back then would have thought of the contemporary Ath-Leisure aesthetic, cheap material and fast fashion made in sweat shops?

As I research the 1970s, I get lost in the ephemera of that time. The photography from Studio 54 may romanticise that party scene, sure . . . but it deeply appeals to the escapist inner-child-full-of-wonder in me, the one who can stare at a mirror ball in pure delight. Oh and, of course Grace hung with Basquait. There is a vibrational photograph of Grace and Basquait, with Nigerian music-making dynamo Fela Kuti, and visual artist Keith

Haring mid-flow of good-times in Mr Chow restaurant in NYC in 1986 that was released by The Andy Warhol Foundation and Jean-Michel estate (to even consider the capturing of photographs in these times is yet another example of how different a lived experience would have been for an artist, there were of course no phones, just a flash of bulb taken and developed by someone else, in a moment where the act of candid photography would likely be forgotten by the subject, this would have affected the psyche).

> Those who demand that you conform the most to how they live are the ones who are the most scared and intimidated by life.
>
> Grace Jones, *I'll Never Write My Memoirs*

Grace has always talked so eloquently about her Jamaican identity. She often describes in interviews how her experiences there as a child and adult have shaped her artistry. In 2022 Grace collaborated with a brand to launch a scented candle called Grace with the tones created from memories of the soil after it rains on the island, infused with hints of 1980s leather, with the aim of evoking the feeling of salt on skin. There's a shared sensuality in two of our three Jamaican Sisters in this hood . . . Una Marson wrote of Jamaica, 'Must have been part of Eden, it's so full of peace and rest.'

In Grace's case it glows in the warmth of her sound, where in many songs you can hear her sing or speak in patois, and sounds bounce lavishly from pop to dub to reggae.

To me, Grace Jones is embodied **sacred geometry**. By this, I mean someone who's designed a life so well that it deserves to be applauded and learnt from. I was delighted to learn, (as sister of the sea myself) that when I interviewed her that she too was a major water enthusiast and swims wherever she goes, preferring the sea for long swims and the local pool for practicing vocals underwater.

> There's a weightlessness that I just love.
>
> Grace, on swimming in the sea

As a child she moved from the island in which she and I share ancestors dwelling on lands not far from one another, to North America, then Paris, London, New York . . . just a few of the places that have been graced with AMAZING . . .

In 1970 Grace moved to Paris and shared a flat with **Jerry Hall** and **Jessica Lange**. Imagine a world where couture, bohemia, and irreverence collided regardless of your background. That was Paris. Paris was where designers, writers, fashionistas and dreamers sought a haven in the early 1970s. Post-1960s delirium was setting in across Europe and Paris was the epicentre for libertarians from all over the world. Those who wanted 'in' on this level of heady glamour descended on the whimsical, courtyard/boulangerie/French-kiss-filled and most overtly romantic city in the world of the time. Grace was 'in' all right, in the IN crowd, and regularly got nude at castings, which the glitterati adored (and which she told me she had zero regrets or embarrassment about).

Grace's pictures of these times (1971–1978) are resplendent and incandescent. She exudes power and pride and most importantly seems to be having the biggest laugh, despite being just at the start of her decades-long career. She is daring to have fun with wildness, nakedness, fashion and total brilliance. She clearly brought this out of others too.

Her sense of agency was contagious, and her ebullient assuredness rippled through her career, right through to today, where her infamous hula-hooping still enraptures audiences in their twenties. Perhaps more than anything, Grace has been an emblem of living life fearlessly and to the full. I remember asking her at one point what it was like to be at Studio 54.

She told me about having the space to twirl and swirl the night away with souls from all walks of life, from the elderly eccentrics of Manhattan still wanting to get dressed to the nines and dance into the eternity that the disco club scene provided, to the gorgeous queers of the night who allowed her to live out her fantasies and be adored as the queen she is. The queen you can see in the black and white photography of Studio 54, in that era, in images of her arriving on a motorbike for her thirtieth birthday with golden shimmer eyes, strappy sandals and not much else except for an entourage of gorgeous folk baring equal amounts of shiny skin, images where she was getting body-painted by her friend and prolific artist Keith Haring in preparation for a night out on the town, ones where she makes shapes gallivanting with fellow stars of the scene in leotards paired with shades, striking poses in hats spouting feathers, those timeless images of her performing on elevated platforms in reams of gold lurex, silken-looking hoods attached her outfits, a boxing belt complete with gloves, with backing dancers in g-strings. Every visual vibrates with an acute attention to detail in an era when there was less rush and more time to get ready and to care as much about celebrating life with splendour and candour as getting through it.

In November of 1979, Grace was pregnant with her first child, and navigated the potential loss of work for a pregnant woman who was a major name on the downtown club scene, by designing cardboard maternity costumes that disguised her bump with her then partner **Jean-Paul Goude** and fashion illustrator Antonio Lopez. This meant performing dressed like a conceptual, asymmetric vase with a graphic triangular hat with an exclamation mark on it! She went on to have the baby in November of that year, and by early 1980 was in the Bahamas recording her album *Warm Leatherette*! If I could interview her again, I would want to know whether she found a similar creative momentum from becoming a mother, as I have.

The album (her fourth) was produced by reggae legends **Sly Dunbar** and **Robbie Shakespeare** and was a huge success, an example of her first foray in experimenting with a multitude of sounds. New-wave, post-punk, funk and reggae are just a few of the amalgamated sonics you experience when you listen to it. Lyrically it's made of a stark power. In the third track – 'Rolling Stone', she paints a cautionary tale of living a life as a 'rolling stone' and implies that if you move too quickly something may be lacking from your life and that it's hard to find love if you're lost. The final track – 'Breakdown' is cover originally written by Tom Petty and the Heartbreakers in 1976, and who even sometimes weaved Ray Charles' 'Hit The Road Jack' (from 1960) into performances of the song. I have such deep affection for the journey of musical legacy, it's such a magical expression of creativity. My god, what I'd do to be able to sing . . . I imagine how it would feel to be just a few months post-partum on a Carribbean island, making music with my friends. It must've been (like so many parts of Grace's life) amazing.

By 1984 she posed ironically naked again, this time with her partner at that time – Dolph Lundgren – for *Playboy*. The pictures are incredible, like all pictures of Grace they are art.

In 1985 Grace played May Day the James Bond film of the time *A View to a Kill*, where her androgynous image broke the mold of expectation once again and her character was a bodyguard and assassin.

I wonder how one conjures such confidence. Is not being afraid of ritualising how we experience fun a path to being our true selves? Is the 'erotic' that Sister Audre invites us to think about (p.73) when it comes to our work and practices striking again here? Within the life of Grace?

When we met, it was 2017 and Grace Jones was wearing the most exquisite boiler suit; high-spec, expensive looking, full of intricate zips and intergalactic allure, complete with a 1940s-esque pilot's hat, the type to have flaps on the ears. She wore no makeup and oozed luminosity and spellbinding beauty. 'This is my flying outfit,' she giggled and gestured to her headwear. 'I wear it because it has pockets. Pockets for my passport, my ticket . . . and I love it when I walk onto the plane because people think I might be flying it because of the hat!' She twinkled with a precious charm. 'They just don't make them like this anymore,' I thought of her contagious mischief.

'What do you fear the most, Grace?' I asked with genuine intrigue, feeling as though I was falling in love.

'The only thing I fear is fear itself,' she replied, echoing the famous **FDR** quote. She then ordered prawns and asked me why I wasn't taking up the offer of a glass of wine.

'Well, I'm working you see, and I never . . . drink . . . when I'm . . .'

'Oh darlingggg,' she replied, 'Red before bed and white to be all right'.

In awe of her constitution and mantra, I joined her. How could I resist that invitation? In the most fabulous setting, a riverbank restaurant on a summer's evening, and the most delicious glass of Sancerre I think I will ever experience in my life.

That's the whole point . . . To get rid of the fear.

Grace, on talking about being part of the acid trials

When we spoke about her being part of the acid trials in our interview, she made a point of explaining how she didn't see the experience in any way as exploitative, because the craziest thing the entire experience led to was . . . her eating ice cream in the nude. I like to think that way of being has stayed with her until now.

Out of all the souls I've interviewed for work, there's one who elicits a universal, kinetic reaction when I mention their name: that person is Grace. Eyes twinkle, excitement is visible and audible, when I mention that I've been in her presence. I wonder if it's the same phenomenon – in reverse – that I detected when I researched Pamela Colman Smith: how writers othered her in their documentation of her, depicting her as a 'creature' of sorts to diminish her power, when secretly / unconsciously they were desperately envious of how authentic / wild / fulfilled she was, they were most certainly drawn to her all the same. That's the effect I think Grace has on people. Except now everyone wants to be her. Or at least be near her. And for one evening in that restaurant I was, sat with her talking. I learnt to love Grace Jones.

> I am disco but I'm also **dada**. I'm a sensualist but also a surrealist. That underground spirit – from the Beats, hippies, civil rights pioneers, punks; from the experimental artists, technicians and designers – dissolved into what became known as independent, as alternative, and that's become less and less subversive, and less resistant to a co-opting commercial pull.
>
> Grace Jones, *I'll Never Write My Memoirs,* 2015

A Sense Memory: On beauty; a remembering; contortion

A woman aged 30 doesn't realise that she's maybe not even halfway through her full and vividly lived life. She lives for the moment and the next 10 minutes. It's a hard and fast way to live that keeps her hot and full of fyah, like lava. She wants to ooze zest and chases honey-dewed glamour through gossip and fashion. Though she is often not in her body, she is truly aware of it. She feels exhaustion for all the flying sleeps in sweat and pimples and her hopeful mind feels drained like a wrung mop for the snakes and ladders of rumour and the internet, Catherine Wheels of success according to the rags // This is the Up and the Down, Chumbawamba once sang about. Reality TV, though guilty, is a pleasure. She sometimes feels guilty, but not for the pleasures, more for the unexplainable way she treats herself and how she bats away negative thoughts with acts of escapism, trying to live gorgeously in the male gaze and other adrenalines. When she was in her teens, it was the adrenaline of getting into nightclubs underage and under disco lights, and DJs on microphones offering free drinks, the rave culture she was too young to experience in its heyday, the titillation of ladette culture and boob jobs / approaching her twenties it was the rock 'n' rolling of braless supermodels and paparazzi shots of everyone famous and celebrated, smoking cigarettes. She cackles about how important these references were to her once but is lost at sea in the scandals of her heroes. It's why she lives for the moment and is strong enough to laugh about the past. It's why she is squeezing her waist into a corset made of rubber called a 'waist trainer' because she can take pain, and it's gain – surely she can be super/sub/human? She believes the targeted advert that promises the tiniest of waists and illusional fat redistributed to other parts of the body where it's desired to create an hourglass figure that the internet ludicrously suggests is possible / She just has to squeeze herself into it first. Clip hook 'n' eyes tightly and angst will disappear, she will be like Jessica Rabbit and harness sex appeal with steely overtness and everything will be better than OK. She squeezes and squeals and asks a friend to help. She squeezes, she kneads, her flesh like dough, breathes in, stops breathing, grits through the demoralisation, it'll all be worth it in the end. After around 60 seconds of agony-and-hope, for the outline of the world's most desired, she gives up and feels like she has been dropped into the trash for trying. What a clown she must be for having bought a rubber waist trainer. It's sadism and lunacy combined for the sake of what? Something she'll ask herself for a long time.

Give GRACE

How was Grace Jones able to find and tend to her fearlessness? Something to do with the era when she was brought up perhaps? When people weren't necessarily exposed to as much hypocrisy and to such confusing messages? I think it's also how she has been celebrated in the circles of some of the greatest artists, proving that if you find your community and keep an eye on what public attention might do to your self-esteem in reality then maybe you'll be able to retain a sense of your true self with pride. When I interviewed her, she told me about discussing culture with Andy Warhol back in the day, when she was not interested in being recognised or garnering attention. She didn't agree to a picture of us together on the day, either, because she wasn't camera ready. I remember being disappointed not to be able to get a photo to mark this pivotal assignment for me, but nearly a decade later I'm really happy it's locked in my memory in a way that can't be diluted by visual evidence. I have an immortal recording instead and am forced to think a little deeper and in a more sensory way about the experience over just the 'accolade' of a photo. How incredible – how inspiring – that someone so comfortable with being photographed is actually (but of course!) in total control of it. She is doing anything but conforming to the idea that everything needs to be captured in such a way. Maybe we could all learn from that? It leads me to ask the question, are we experiencing a moment completely differently when not picturing it? Are we placing the memory internally somewhere else altogether differently?

Where would you go, if the practicality or your current circumstances / the way you were brought up weren't an issue? How would you express yourself if you weren't comparing yourself to anyone else, but only by the standard of your most free and wild dreams?

A Sense Memory: Coming to Edinburgh

My partner and I came on a wing and a prayer, in March 2021. Well, actually, in a Fiat Panda that I'd bought on Facebook Marketplace for 500 quid. She was called Tina after Tina Turner. We packed Tina with stuff, I have a lot of it, which I may have mentioned already. Trinkets, lamps, sequinned gowns, stools, enough to make me old-fashioned in a minimalist, understated and clean-cut Instagrammable world, but really it's old-fashioned in a way that I'm more than comfortable with. I felt ALIVE, I felt in real love, I felt euphoric, for having survived a Global Pandemic, that I thought I might die at the start of . . . it would either have been grief, the virus, or general Armageddon – either way, I had definitely endured nightmares that had now subsided. The world wasn't ending and there we were – now there were two of us – driving northwards, and into our unknown future and it felt like shades of the void were brightening and the worst was over and changing . . . into something NEW. It was refreshment for my nervous system as well as my career path. Why Edinburgh? We get asked that a lot. Well, funnily enough, two years earlier, as I was looking out the window of my month-long temporary accommodation in Edinburgh in 2019 (before the pandemic changed everything), when I had been working in the city producing a punk coming-of-age musical called *Parakeet* about climate change written by one of my best friends – **Brigitte Aphrodite** – and I had found myself looking out my apartment window and noticing the warm glow of a very smart flat across the road and how candles flickered and beautiful abstract paintings hung on the wall, and I was having such a good time that summer – I'd been strutting about the place, feeling connected to so much good cultural activity but not owned by any of it, dipping in and out of working for the International Book Festival producing an interesting offering on the Fringe circuit, DJ'd at a friend's drag night – it had meant feeling part of many cultural tribes, it had meant landing in the centre of a cultural quilt, undefined by one particular institution, and finally having autonomy.

I was also swimming all the time, because I was missing my chilled sea dips in Margate where I was living in my own flat, so I settled for the local Edinburgh Leisure Pool instead, a place pleasingly called Glenogle (sounds a bit like **bogle**) Swim Centre, one of the city's many frankly beautiful buildings made accessible with affordable entry and huge ceiling windows, where I floated on the water letting the light flood my senses, leaving me feeling like I could be whoever I wanted to be, anything was possible and that life when in-flow, when swimming, was such a gift. And it wasn't just the swimming. I'd got the opportunity to chair a conversation with the electrifyingly brilliant **Benjamin Zephaniah** that month, which he wrapped up by singing **Bobby McFerrin**'s 'Don't Worry, Be Happy', and a member of the audience screamed how they wanted him to be their Prime Minister, not knowing all that was to come for their actual Prime Minister, and that Benjamin Zephaniah would pass away unexpectedly four years later. I'd eaten great food that summer and appreciated the scholarly nature of all the university buildings. I was starting to realise Edinburgh is full of a timeless magic, not quite the same as anywhere else in the world. It was in that lucid moment, looking out the window and into someone else's home across the street, that I put out a wish to the fae.

'When I grow up, I'd like to be a writer and live in Edinburgh.'

So I decided to move after that summer of 'solo & single' love. Little did I know that a year later I'd have truly, madly, deeply fallen for the guy who I'd met atop a Malawian mountain and that we would head to live in Scotland together, having both survived the introduction to a global pandemic, and that although we had been exposed to much ending of life and fear and were right to distrust so much of what was put to us as 'sensible' and 'conventional', it was all so topsy-turvy and mad that radical acts of love felt like the only way of life. So after having discussed how we both had Scottish ancestry (my maternal grandparents – Margaret and Jim – were both from Glasgow, and his great-grandfather Syd had been born there too) and how we both found deep solace in epic and monumental nature, decided not to put too much pressure on ourselves . . . just cling to the wing and say a prayer that our guts and the ghosts were right, that there might be a chance to do some growing up here, that the rumours that the culture were as inviting as they seemed, that we could head as far away from Westminster as possible in order to have sublime nature in our eyes rather than be clouded by the blur of a proximity to parliament and gentrification and the rising prices of just about everything . . . to try something new. It turns out of all of things that felt new, there was also going to be an intense embracing of the dark of winters, and remembering that this was in fact where I'd first dreamed of becoming a writer (even if I didn't yet know it was also going to mean pivoting to being artist too) because other work would dry up for some time. I could carry on swimming up here and could perhaps grow, using the techniques and tools I'd had to learn of late after a somewhat unwieldy childhood, but now without the infantilisation of being in the public eye and in Broadcast since my early twenties. I could come at it now from a wiser perspective and just perhaps be taken seriously in a stomping ground for the curious and the progressive, for explorers and descendants of archaeologists. I was no longer 'the girl that presented the roving reportage on the BBC at Glastonbury' who wore fairy wings and guffawed and hung around indie bands. I had travelled the world, found healing in the quiet, I wanted to grow up and I was in LOVE.

The adventures continue, because Scotland is endless and full of folklore, witchery and a heritage when it comes to so much of my passion. We dip into the seas here and they are colder than those of the South East, more immediate. We enterprise and learn here. I have become the writer I felt the call to be and we gave birth to our first baby here.

19 March 2021

A new place to live in Scotland, broken bones

Dear Sister Grace

I'm writing this from my new gorgeous flat in Marchmont, Edinburgh. So much of life is sparkling and new and exciting. I've fallen in love with a very laid back handsome nature-man called Cameron. He works with coffee farmers and as a hobby has trained as a boxer and has even done one professional fight. I remember you telling me you once spent some time learning boxing? Did you spar with anyone? I find even the thought so dangerous. Right now, though, in a mad twist of fate on the third day of living here . . . my boyfriend and I went to walk up Arthur's Seat (a big hill here that used to be an active volcano, around 340 million years ago), a hike I absolutely love and have done many times before on visits to the city. But now I live here, and I thought it would be a romantic thing to do, as it was his 30th birthday, and there aren't many other options as we're all locked down due to this seemingly everlasting pandemic and . . . I broke my leg. In three places. Slipped in the rain and tried to get up too quickly, in fear of looking like a fool, which I only became more of, as I hurt myself so badly. I knew it was serious straight away and clasped my ankle real tight and told him to ring for an ambulance. It felt insane. We've all been told not to come near one another outside our bubbles so even though I was clearly hurt, most other people walked on. Anyway, I had to go straight to hospital. It wasn't quite far up enough for a helicopter, so I hopped with one hand on my boyfriend's shoulder and the other on a paramedic's.

I'm still in shock. I was so strung out by the gas and air that I started to try and wisecrack with a deeper voice than usual, as though I was an ole-timey blues singer! I also found the doctors' double act of putting on my plaster cast one of the most tender, loving acts I've ever seen. I watched as they communicated softly and bound my leg to a position of healing. It felt warm, and they seemed like they were ballet dancing (I was still high from the various meds) and I told them so in a melodramatic thank you. So now it's my birthday (yeah, I forgot to add that . . . it's Cameron on the 15th and mine on the 19th!) and I have been operated on. They've stuck some titanium into my right leg and I have a giant heavy moon boot, but I'm discharged and home in our new rented tenement flat in Marchmont and I've just turned 36. What a madness . . . Have you ever injured yourself and been forced to rest and recover? I'll never forget our interview together and your sense of fearlessness. You told me about your love of swimming, a pastime I was yet to develop with as full velocity as I did! I ended up falling in love with cold-water sea swimming. I would love to sea swim with you.

So that's been my welcome to Scotland. And now I'm set to spend some months on crutches. But I'm finding them so hard to walk on. I feel so weak. Today, as it was my birthday, Cameron found me a set of wheels (a wheelchair) on Gumtree so that we could go to the beach and I could whizz down the promenade in a party dress at least.

There's a myth in Scottish folklore called the Cailleach: a

giant of a woman sculpted into the landscape of Scotland. She is the 'Queen of Weather' and controls how harsh the winters will be. She roams with a huge staff, that she taps into the earth to create springs of water, mountains and valleys. Thank you, Cailleach, for reminding us how we as womxn are living **almanacs**, marking changes as powerful as weather.

Have you ever come across an equivalent in Jamaican folklore? I think she might be you.

Chapter Threads

Jerry Hall – American model and actress.

Jessica Lange – American actress and photographer.

Jean-Paul Goude – French graphic designer and illustrator.

Sly Dunbar and **Robbie Shakespeare** – Sly & Robbie are prolific and magnetic Jamaican musicians, mostly known as a music production duo. Sly was born in 1952 and Robbie in 1953.

FDR quote – Franklin D. Roosevelt was the US president in 1933 and used this phrase in his inaugural speech during a time of Great Depression.

Dada – an anarchic underground art scene coined 'dada' in Europe in 1916. Dada emerged from an urgency to forge radical visual and literary collage by merging genre and form and creating absurdist and non-sensical commentary in protest to the horrors and momentous nationalism of World War I.

Brigitte Aphrodite – a wonderful contemporary punk, feminist showgirl, writer and theatre maker.

bogle – a folkloric goblin or scarecrow in Scotland or a wicked dance move that involved creating huge circles with your arms whilst whinin' and pointing your fingers in Jamaica.

Benjamin Zephaniah – a wordsmith, author, reggae artist, activist and legend born in Birmingham in 1953.

Bobby McFerrin – a conductor, improvisational musician and legend born in New York City in 1953.

almanacs – a calendar holding the important dates and junctures. Often of tide tables or moon phases.

Snake Beat PT V

Trans-cend
Translate
Re-late, Translate,
des-cribe,
Re-birth,
Re-form.

7

Marsha P. Johnson

Butterfly of style and expression

'Orchids love me, they thrive around me'

Marsha, on her favourite flowers

Born: 24 August 1945, Elizabeth, New Jersey, United States
Died: 6 July 1992, New York, United States
Sign: Virgo
Pronouns: She / Her

Marsha P. Johnson, an African American gay liberation activist and self-identified drag queen. The P in her name stood for 'Pay It No Mind'. She was so many things in such a short amount of time: a living zeitgeist, a firework, performer and dreamer.

A queer trans woman who became known during the late 1960s scene in New York for her charm, her dazzling displays of style, her huge smile, her laughter, and her activism that provided safety for the most marginalised, underrepresented and brutalised. She was remembered – most important to note – for her fierce sense of friendship.

They call me a legend in my own time because there were so many queens gone that I'm one of the few queens left from the 70s and the 80s.[1]

Queersticity; A necessity of queer

In the English dictionary, the first meaning of queer is 'odd', before any meaning to do with a person's sexuality. Oddness is an area that has followed me my whole life. I've always tried to subvert what's expected of me, something I've often tried to escape by countering it with being preposterously 'colourful' instead. I've also learned that it's when I am with queer hearts that I feel the most seen and forgiven for not being able to think in a way that is considered 'normal'. *Queer* being the operative word, and meaning many things. An eye that is all-loving and in love with love and in balance outweighs everything: austere systems, a lacklustre sense of doom. I see the sun as queer, plants in the tropics as queer, laughter in sex as queer, the moment our bodies ride a beat in time when on a dance floor as queer, experimentation outside of any box as queer, all these things as wonderful and necessary and a framework and history that should be nurtured and brought into all light.

Marsha was born in a small town in New Jersey, one of a brood of seven children in a very religious household in the African Methodist Episcopal (A.M.E.) Church. Her mother was cited as saying that being gay is an 'act lower than a dog's.'

Marsha said that in those days, the idea of being gay seemed like 'a sort of dream', a dream worthy of pulling into reality. Changing her name from the one she was born with – Malcolm Michaels Jr. – to the soon-to-be-renowned 'Marsha P.'; she moved with just 15 dollars and a bag of clothes, aged 17, to New York City. It was 1963.

> Guilt and defensiveness are bricks in a wall against which we will all perish, for they serve none of our futures.
>
> Audre Lorde

In 1967, four years later, Nina Simone (who was living in New York at the same time) released 'Don't You Pay Them No Mind', a heart-breaking ballad that describes a particular strength of love in someone forced to tolerate other people's intolerance of them existing. It's a love song about resilience that reminds us that pure love as a force cannot be stopped even if others 'laugh and point at you' as in the lyrics. I can't help but link it to the resilience in Marsha's legacy. The fact that even the simple placement of 'P.' in her name asks of us to take her as she is – to accept her identity as multifaceted, fallible, trans, human, fierce and full of soulful love – is activism at its most nuanced. It reminds us that names are as erasable as all trans-centred history and demands of us to think about where and how hatred and judgement poke out of our humanity and can intrude a society's mind.

Marsha & Sylvia – the brave-hearts

Moonlighting as a sex worker to make a living, and despite being charged over a hundred times with criminality for such work, Marsha was an indispensable figure of her time, affectionately known as 'Black Marsha' among her community. There's a scene in the documentary *The Death and Life of Marsha P. Johnson* of archival footage where she interacts with acquaintances on the streets of Manhattan back in the 1970s, and her vibe cannot be mistaken. She has a spellbinding presence, the kind that is resonant even on tape. She beams with a warmth and wit that intuitively makes me wish I could have met her in person and explains why so many of the East Coast queer community of America who knew her still light up when they talk about the effect she had on them. There are documents of her lasting impact in the roots of most LGBTQ+ movements. Marsha P's phenomenon continues to create a bedrock of liberty and protection for the most vulnerable. Some of the photography alone is the most radiant and spellbinding capturing of this scene in this time.

There's a lot of myth and legend around the circumstances that led to the infamous Stonewall Inn uprising in Greenwich Village in late June 1969, known today as the Stonewall Riots. We know they happened as a retaliation to the violence and harm to which the gay community was often subjected. Gay bars and gatherings in the area had been repeatedly raided and shut down, queer sex workers had been regularly beaten and even murdered. The laws didn't recognise same-sex love and the stigma surrounding queer sexuality was egregious for too many. The queer community's anguish over all this was enough for the riots to last five days. After the NYPD, dressed in plain clothes, raided another gay bar, this time all hell broke loose. The number of people protesting and rioting doubled from one day to the next. Stonewall changed the queer landscape for ever. One version of events has it that Marsha began it all, and that Marsha and her best friend, Latinx drag queen Sylvia Rivera (a member of the Immortal hood in her own right), were the ones who threw the first stones. A rallying cry for a safe lived existence.

When humans stand up with their bodies, and relentlessly, physically demand liberation, it's born from necessity, defiance and demand. Years of physical and mental abuse had been endured by LGBTQI+ people in 1969, even in a congregational, queer explosion of a place such as NYC.

> History isn't something you look back at and say it was inevitable, it happens because people make decisions that are sometimes very impulsive and of the moment, but those moments are cumulative realities.
>
> Marsha P. Johnson

For some time she was known as the 'Mayor of Christopher Street', so loved and welcoming a presence in the streets of Greenwich village was she.

Today there is enough spirited honouring of Marsha and her love that you can make a pilgrimage to a luscious, waterfront, seven-acre park in Brooklyn, New York City named Marsha P. Johnson State Park. Singer **Anohni**'s album, released in 2023 – *My Back Was a Bridge for You to Cross* – pays tribute to Marsha's plea for human rights. The songs on this album act as a gentle confrontation and antidote to the vitriol and swell of hatred for our trans family. Tracks such as 'It Must Change', 'Scapegoat' and 'Why Am I Alive Now?' from the album, I believe, should be played loudly into angry, loud crowds of racist and transphobic gangs // the songs are alliances – offering sonic lullaby to the hurt folk. I cried when I listened to Anohni's album in full. I wondered how I could continue the legacy of Marsha and Sylvia's work in my lifetime and how I could ever do it with as much grace as this music, and how I could stand in solidarity with all living bodies who have been subjected to rejection in society for who they are.

> The generosity of Marsha's spirit. She was a mother. She mothered so many young queer, trans and gender non-conforming

people and that was so important to her. And she talked time and time again about how much she wanted to reach her hand out when other people aren't. Another thing is that in that moment, they were hustling in order to rent these hourly hotels. They used to call them 'hot spring' hotels because whether it was summer, spring, winter, fall you couldn't open the window and heat was blasting, it was like everyone was sweating. But it was in that context they had a little bit of safety from the police violence and harassment happening downstairs. At the time if you were a trans woman and you weren't wearing three articles of men's clothing you would be arrested and put in jail as a state law in New York State. It wasn't repealed until 2020. Y'know, it wasn't long ago that these 'three articles of clothing' laws were taken off the books in the US. Literally, that's 2020 during the COVID emergence. So to me, it's to just think about how they used that space, that hourly hotel, as a place to dream beyond what is. They were so keenly aware of all of the day-to-day problems and yet their focus in those moments was to imagine beyond them and help each other usher in the world that they deserved. And to me, I always come back to that moment because we're in a similar place of harsh conditions and we cannot go outside, or we cannot open a screen without seeing evidence of that but to me it's so important to do that '**Marsha Magic**' as I call it and use that as an impetus to dream beyond what it is and into the world we want to usher into place.

Tourmaline, a visual artist and biographer of Marsha P. Johnson

I may be crazy, but that don't make me wrong.

Marsha P. Johnson[2]

Marsha navigated myriad mental health-related issues. They increased violently as her life went on, and as she continued to come to terms with the rejection she experienced from so many quarters of society. It wasn't just the police who punished Marsha. It was many who identified as gay men and who didn't respect the role of trans women within the Gay Rights movement. Both Marsha and Sylvia spent so much of their time and energy trying to uplift and protect these women. Towards the late 1970s Marsha often relied on prescribed sedatives and her friends often tried to raise bail money together for the times she ended up in custody after a fight while under the influence of potent prescription drugs. She was shot once, too. Is it any wonder that having to endure that kind of hardship should lead to emotional dysregulation and eventually breakdown?

Marsha was a founding member of the Gay Liberation Front, and a co-founder of the radical activist group Street Transvestite Action Revolutionaries (STAR). Alongside her best friend and confidante Sylvia, Marsha is a revered figure of resistance among the esteemed company of this book. If I hadn't stumbled upon the film about Marsha's life and death, I might not have known about her beyond some great pictures that are shared online sometimes, or been able to connect so deeply with those who fought for trans rights in the 1970s. Why are we not learning about Marsha and Sylvia in schools? Why are they not the subject matter of history podcasts and why is the only widely available resource about her on a streaming platform? Why does it reduce her life to how she died and its brutality? Which leads me to note, that I've noticed so many mainstream documentaries or films about Black women are about their lives ending rather than celebrating all that they did and changed and the legacy of the work they left behind.

Quest for visibility: Sistxr Synchronicity

Is it a curse to yearn to be accepted? I believe it shouldn't be, but those of us who live life on the margins might have to wade through negative thoughts that don't sit comfortably beneath our skin. In a landscape that can so easily be hostile, we are all so often forced to find words to explain how the hatred of racism and misogyny and other forms of bias slowly diminish our capacity for full, energised, heart-led, accepted and resourced lives. Living in spaces where real love holds us in all its layers can be hard. It's only by integrating fully into the complexities of real community and thinking about queer futures that I've found tangible threads of healing from trauma so vast that it can move through generations. Queer identity in its nuance and ambiguity is a source of so much belonging for so many of us. It's the opposite of division. It is an embracing of the present and a celebration of the gift of life through removing the limitations of the binary and patriarchal notions put on us. It's in refuge, rest, dancing, moving through, transition and change that a love lives, something that is so pertinent to the concept of Sistxrhood that I feel alive with hope even in the act of writing it down. Say it out loud, shake, rattle and know that you are safe to be whoever you want to be in this hood.

When I am seen and heard, eye to eye with friends and chosen family and peers, a true sense of self takes hold, with all my contradictions and emotional textures and growth. It is a feeling not found in the validation of 'likes' or quick-hit-trysts but in the breadth and layers of those who know how to support others without discrimination. The quest for recognition, survival and encouragement – to exist, to lift upwards, to write, to create, to shine, to try, to want abundance and safety – are regularly pushed up against the barriers of oppression and the terror of impostor syndrome that arise whenever Western intellectualism berates /

grates and puts us (paradoxically, a global majority) in our place: a place that forces us to address our insecurities and forgive ourselves for our reactions to the normalised harm that is thrown at us when you are 'other'.

I've grown to love the precious quality of the queer, the different and the misfits. I've learned so much from stories of trans people, freedom fighters, activists and relentless healers in their quest to be accepted as equals. I can only bow my head and wish them peace in their lived struggle. I have been brought up a descendant of displaced people. I was born into the generation of 'go getting' data-style success, the flashy capitalist hangover from the 1980s in our collective shadow. But I commit to doing the work that brings me to the importance of civility held up by equity, and now that I have seen all I have seen and heard all I've heard, I feel blessed to be guided by great ghosts, figures of culture shaping a map that's safe for us to reside in. It's in my search for love and pride that I continue that quest.

A Sense Memory: The Rat Race

A woman blinks down the wires of a video call, in slight disbelief at how obviously the man she is speaking to is typing on his keyboard while speaking to her in this scheduled meeting that's been in the diary for weeks. She's there because she wants to pitch him a TV series, a rarity these days, as she chooses to cocoon herself in the solitude of the written word more, now she's nearly 40 and has played the snakes and ladders of a career based on 'looks and personality' for what feels like for ever. This meeting, though, is a result of some gusto and energy for new ideas found on a recent trip to Los Angeles in search of a sunshine injection, a positivity-stir for the soul in February (that would otherwise be spent writing in the **dreich** air of Scotland).

She feels liberated by the dynamism of the women she meets, many of them escaping violence or other forms of harm. One evening she shared oxtail with a group of Black visionaries and relished in the rarity of truth that is the onyx[3] heart of Black wonder and joy. She was inspired by the life-living, the making and creating, the laughter, the pleasure seeking, the well-being, the go-getting, the journeys of the talented folk she met on this trip. She wanted to document it, illustrate it, show credit, lift up, be arm in arm with, play within the safety and springs of progress, migration and pathways that had been presented to her on that particular California trip. She'd come home dazzled and full of the beans of being treated as an equal, allowed to have big dreams and ready to work up a proposal, something she hadn't done in a while since the last spark of idea-energy was rejected at the first hurdle. But both time and sunshine are the best resources of restoration and reparation of broken-heartedness after all.

Here she is, pitching an idea to a top dog at a global company, with nothing to lose. So she thinks, until she feels some of her dignity leave her voice when she notices he's not even willing to have the meeting without typing, seemingly answering emails at the same time as bandying about words heard before but in different orders and noticing a newer co-opting of powerful language since the trend of 'Diversity and Inclusion' training at corporations.

'Your idea is brilliant, but we need numbers,' he explains hurriedly and cites that programmes about premiership footballers are 'doing well'.

'How can you guarantee true diversity of content if you drive your commissioning based on such high numbers?' she queries.

She means stats, popularity, social media numbers / MONEY and how capital-driven the rat race of numbers / numbers, numbers / and our societal obsession is. How the more she thinks about the normalisation of 'greed-core', narcissism, vanity and luxury, the more contortion of the lived experience has been apparent to her. How it is unnatural for storytellers to be told they have to increasingly care about numbers over feeling or effect on the audience. How the art of mass entertainment, mass appeal and the age of austerity interconnect. We need a reset. We are nations of fatigued people, hungry for even our most basic needs. We need options of resistance, bold ideas and access to the arts and philosophy on mainstream platforms to be championed as alternative options to patriarchal, money-making, hatred raising comparison. We need space, protection and care more than we need the startling convenience of Amazon packages.

This is what she wants to say. But she is frozen.

'Oh, Diversity. Thanks for mentioning it. It's important people such as you are "pulling up" people such as me on this,' he says. 'Well, diversity is baked into everything we do.' At this point, the young woman with the ideas and the fire in her belly politely wraps up the meeting with a thank you and goodbye. The laptop is shut down and she roars on her way home, vowing to let the sunshine hit her bones again soon and to not give up trying to get her ideas out there. She tries to remember that on earth there are places where stats, numbers and mass-populism don't matter and she would be too enraptured by the vastness of the landscape around her to worry about the lines starting to appear on her face, the same face that still, every now and then, gets some gusto, some energy, is ready to pitch and try to work with the flow of what's deemed normal.

Resistance and harm

In critical psychologist Guilaine Kinouani's book *Living While Black: The essential guide to overcoming racial trauma*, a number of healing strategies are outlined to overcome the root cause of much common emotional trauma such as microaggresions / unconscious bias that those racialised as Black or brown are exposed to. Reading an academic and well-researched description of what we can be subjected to when being racialised as Black and when we try to resist hatred and inequality makes for an empowering and galvanising read. In a chapter called 'Race Reflections', Guilaine asks the reader to write down their own bodily responses following detailed historical information of white supremacy and oppression in Western medical systems and society dating back to the times of forced slavery. I'm moved to respond and find myself writing.

In people's eyes sometimes,
auras of supremacy sometimes clouding vision,
discombobulating in the lighting of gas,
dizzying,
can create headaches of distress.
Nervous system searches for escape.
Fear to trust.

I think of the times I've taken flight, in an attempt to get rid of the insidious tinges of racism that I've felt directed towards me. Hierarchy and dominance are more baked into our society than the 'drive for diversity' spoken of by the gatekeepers / some movers / some shakers, the authority / the powers that be, while gaslighting us. I care about Marsha's life and her capacity to care so much, as I cannot imagine the treatment of also being trans layering onto the regularity of racism, but the statistics are enough to have me vow my solidarity in the campaigning for trans rights. Right now in the UK, 46 per cent of trans people have thought about taking their own life.

> We do not have to romanticise our past in order to be aware of how it seeds our present. We do not have to suffer the waste of an amnesia that robs us of the lessons of the past rather than permit us to read them with pride as well as deep understanding.
>
> We know what it is to be lied to, and we know how important it is not to lie to ourselves.
>
> Audre Lorde's address 'Learning from the 60s', Malcolm X weekend, Harvard University

A Sense Memory: I hear Groundations when I write

On beautiful unity. Let me tell you about 'Groundations', a tradition practised often in the Caribbean and associated especially with Rastafarian culture, a chance to fuse the beats and chants we carry from our African ancestors. A number of percussion instruments are used in these gatherings called Nyahbingi rhythms, with the 'repeater' as it's known or 'Kete' taking a more improvisational and 'in the moment' role during the 'groundation ceremony'. The 'repeater' is a small, higher pitched drum than others used in this practice and is seen as the carrier of spirit. The sounds and psalms of Nyahbingi can be traced to tribes and kingdoms in Ghana and Nigeria, and combine themes of reparation and Black redemption. The world reverberates to the heartbeat at the core of this communication, when we move in the cacophonies created in Ska, Reggae and Rocksteady music – often influenced and layered versions of Groundations that have travelled hundreds of years.

If the dance floor has not healed me in moments, then I'm not sure what has. I've been lucky enough to worship in body over mind. Vibration from ground, forgiving us all, limb by limb, groove by groove, twirl by twirl.

Dandelions growing at our feet, not as weeds but healing, mini suns sun bursting, yellow flower that grows naturally even in harsh conditions

apothecary's and divination practitioners know that where it grows, it brings positive energy.

Redemption sounds

It is thought that Johnson never self-identified with the term transgender, but the term was also not in broad use at the time Johnson was alive. Johnson's style of drag was gloriously DIY due to the fact that she was unable to afford clothing from expensive stores. Johnson received leftover flowers after sleeping under tables used for sorting blooms in the Flower District of Manhattan, and was known for wearing crowns of fresh flowers. Johnson was tall, slender and often dressed in flowing robes and shiny dresses, red plastic high heels and bright wigs, which tended to draw attention.

I wonder if those of us that dream of better futures adorn ourselves abstractly in the face of harm. Do flowers in our hair soften the potential of threat? Othered, marginalised and abused, Marsha stayed firmly in her position of resistance until the close of her abruptly-ended time on earth. Adorned in textures and shapes, flamboyance, elegance and beauty.

In 1970 Marsha P. Johnson and her best friend Sylvia set up a safe house and sanctuary called STAR House, a shelter for homeless LGBTQI+ folk. Before they secured the building, they'd run a less official safe house in a trailer truck for trans youth in Greenwich village. Marsha and Sylvia knew that the trans community had been somewhat forgotten in the fight for gay rights. For trans people in Manhattan, those who had been outcast from society were able to experience home and sanctuary at Marsha and Sylvia's shelter. It wasn't safe for them to be in existence then, nor was it safe to resist in acts of nurture, when the environment was one of such hardness. Institutional support and financing networks weren't available for STAR, the trans voice not deemed valuable enough to encourage. My heart cracks when I watch Sylvia Rivera scream for care of trans rights at the 1973 Gay Pride rally in NYC. 'I have been beaten, I have been thrown in jail, I have lost my job, I have lost my apartment, for gay liberation and you all treat me this way' she screams in disbelief into the microphone at the crowds booing her.

To imagine what it must have taken to come up against these attitudes and stay upright leaves me in awe. Fear didn't win in this mission. The service Marsha and Sylvia provided at STAR was desperately needed by the most vulnerable people. They spent so much of their time answering phone calls from people in need of protection who had been cast out on the street.

> It is not a joke nor anything to make light of. Black people dying from sleep deprivation and our resistance to rest is a social justice and public health issue.
>
> Tricia Hershey, author and founder of the Nap Ministry, 2022

In the 1980s, Johnson continued to play an active part in street activism as a respected organiser and marshal with the Aids activism group ACT UP. In 1992, when the first **Gay Liberation**

monument was moved to Christopher Street from Ohio to recognise the gay liberation movement, Johnson commented,

> How many people have died for these two little statues to be put in the park to recognise gay people? How many years does it take for people to see that we're all brothers and sisters and human beings in the human race? I mean, how many years does it take for people to see that we're all in this rat race together?

We stand on the shoulders of Marsha. The pioneers and trans-trailblazers of our times all have Marsha and her connection to Sylvia and the setting up of the STAR house to learn from. For their legacies live in our innate need and want for love. In the flowers that we decorate our countertops with and get delivered to our friends and peers, in gestures of cheer and condolences. They are in the exquisite display of warrior-ism when we apply accentuating makeup. Red lips for affectionate and passionate thoughts and lucky kisses, drag queen pearls, and accessories purely for the enjoyment and splendour of our bodies as art.

I'm captivated by the trans community and respect the reverberant resistance of queer culture around the world. If collective liberation is on our agenda, then we're in for a ride – a roller coaster of de-stigmatisation of the complexities of our mental health must unfold and we need to start seeing ourselves as humans in vital need of liberation from chains and hate, some of it conditioned, if not 'baked' internally and disguised as a status quo. I know some of the kindest, most gentle and creative souls to be those of my trans friends. I owe them so much, for they have guided and taught me about so many things. They have shown me a path of self-discovery like no other beings.

In 2023, Anohni put out her album *My Back Was a Bridge for You to Cross* as an ode to the angelic nature and work of Marsha P. Johnson. She described her honouring of Marsha with words of sweetness and reverence and wrote a description of the day she wore a wedding dress to Marsha's commemoration. The recognition and love for Marsha and her sister Sylvia ignited a truth beneath my skin. Community and love are everything. Lauryn Hill once sang of it in her arias to everything. Everything is everything.

Mustering active resistance

I've had the privilege of finding time to sit with my body and soul and work out, in a stark modern light, what serves or harms me. It is only through reading, writing, art and educating myself as an adult that I have been able to put in place my very own path, outside of the societal pressure which I've found to encourage a type of contortion that is crushingly normalised. It is outside of genres and the barriers of over-explanation that I've found I really flourish. I do get tired sometimes, and then, well, then I run to the sea. I can only imagine how much hostility a transperson may face everyday.

I will walk beside you. Let us wish into bodies of water . . .

Let us say our wishes and dreams into bodies of water . . .

I felt humbled to be in conversation on stage in the summer of 2023 with the effervescent model, writer and trans rights activist Munroe Bergdorf. Munroe's words during the conversation hung in the air like the charge that huge thunderstorms set in the atmosphere, her ideas creating **lightning bolts in a crowd** listening so intently that I could almost feel the atmosphere of poignancy and crackles of opening up from the people who had given themselves time just to listen to someone's lived experience, as we are in the room together. 'We need more trans stories' she said, 'we have always been there, we will always be here, we are here and we are just trying to live'. Munroe spoke of the horrors and threats trans people are subjected to when their lives are bandied around as 'talking points' on Breakfast TV and rolling news feeds. I can empathise with the sensationalism of the media.

I want to uphold the lives of trans women as much as I do any socialised and identifying womxn in *The Immortal Sisterhood*. Our womanhood is immortal and it's an honour to archive the threads of the life's work of Marsha P. Johnson.

Creating home can be a sacred act. Especially when there are so many factors at play, trying to prevent you from the rest needed to survive fully, sanctity is necessity for the vulnerable especially. Below, bell hooks speaks of home in the most perfect of ways, and in a way that only bell hooks can encapsulate:

> Creating domestic bliss is especially useful for individuals living alone who are just learning to be self-loving. When we intentionally strive to make our homes places where we are ready to give and receive love, every object place there enhances our well-being.
>
> bell hooks – *all about love: new visions*

A Sense Memory: Encased in pink

I keep dreaming of my teenage bedroom. It was bright pink; its given name by the paint company was 'Sexy Pink'. I painted it myself, with determined gangly teen arms and a paint roller. Even the ceiling was the shade of excitable flamingo. At the time I desired 'cheap going-out-tops', showgirls' feather boas and plastic accessories – Sexy Pink was perfect, I wanted to be encased in the hue. What is it about the delight in our chosen aesthetic being achieved, and how do we choose the colours of the walls we live inside and wear on our bodies? In colour magic theory, pinks and reds represent romance and our heart.

Stonewall was a rising-up, a sudden burst of momentum in a protest that had been running a long time. Gay rights, in a place as gay as New York, had to happen – the streets were exploding with a need for humanitarian equilibrium – but to the visible shock of the trans community, it was clear that their lives, dreams and minds were not seen as vital to save.

I'm ready to ritualise and practise positivity over brutality, because I am free.

I understand freeness, I am free, there is freedom in my blood, I hold freedom in my dance, in my bones, I understand freeness.

Our liberation is interconnected.

I am free.

And I wouldn't have known how free I was, unless Marsha showed me how radical freeness is, I thank you and I love you. Would Marsha have been able to trailblaze in a world of click-bait anti-transness? I actually think that she would have, yes. But I would argue that there might be more Marshas bringing joy if we hadn't got to a place where we stifle our imagination, don't go out much, are afraid to interrogate our collective lethargy. When once boredom and even disenfranchisement may have manoeuvred us into a space where we became 'out-there' magpies and master inventors, that same boredom and disenfranchisement is now vampire-sucked into the pockets of the hoarding and the wealthy who run mega corporations. You can't buy the integrity of resistance despite the co-opting of activist language by politicians who want you to vote for them, or social media sites designed to hold you to psychological ransom in hashtag form.

I want to socialise in all the world's mess and physical nature. I want to dance with you through fear, and dress up to the nines in cocktail attire, and make headpieces out of feathers and flowers. I want to subvert industrialism into **Gaia** philosophy. I want to live in a community with care and imagination as its intention. I wish for Marsha's legacy to thrive and for the rest of us to find our humanity in hers.

A thought for the family I chose / a note on radical friendship

We thought we'd all be down the road from one another. Floating on momentum and the moment, knocking on one another's doors to socialise. Squished into the folds of a sofa, with mutual running commentary of the TV as we fossilised, got older. Took over dance floors euphorically into our thirties, forties, fifties, like we did in our twenties. But what happened? Now we meet once a year in person and spend the cost of living / lit up by the light of our WhatsApp groups, pleading with our diaries to have a time in sync with our friends who we want to commune with most. The fellowship, the people you want to be arm in arm with on any ship that was to go down. The hearts of some that lift you up when you're broken and hug you into a new day without risk of resentment. Chosen families . . . But we were outpriced. Austerity took this romance from our future. I miss you.

July 2025

Dear Martha

I'm on a Scottish Island, called the Isle Of Mull, I've brought an ensemble-led piece of avant garde theatre here, which feels hysterical! As if the outer Hebrides weren't ethereal and surreal enough already without our chanting and ritual, but that's the whole point . . . With this project I feel compelled to move with it, not be bound by conventional expectation. Sometimes it feels so hard to RE-JOICE and to reclaim joy in the survival of this world and to exist within the nature of liminal grief that crowds our consciousness in these challenging times. To know that you went too soon is such a deep sadness to me. To know how much you inspired so many, though, is warming and I want to thank you for your commitment to care, to sanctuary and continuous thinking of ways to make others feel lifted and seen, despite such lack of material resource it is obvious that there was much love that poured from you. When I feel hope starting to fade from grasp, I remember how much you struggled and yet stayed resilient and never gave up. Your end came too soon. But the life you led – so beautifully and gracefully – right up to that moment, continues to give energy and strength to many of us.

I can't stop thinking about how I'd like to drink tea with you, tell you of all the pervasive fear a lot of us feel, the tendency to both dizzyingly bombard and blame anyone but ourselves about all the pain in today's society, and I wonder how it might have compared to your life of extremes in a grit-filled New York in the 70s? I'm 40 as I write this; you lived to 46.

What did you do for your 40th? I feel you would be proud of your beautiful community now. So many thriving transfolk despite unequal rights and discrimination, of all the people I know my trans friends are always the most dynamic at finding ways to live lives of art and love, two things I see to be eternally connected.

In the biography about your life, *Marsha, The Joy and Defiance of Marsha P. Johnson* – written by the incredible Tourmaline, she describes how you used to perform in Aids hospices and hospitals and how you saw performance as an act of radical nurture. I wept, when I read that, because if everyone that entertained saw this responsibility and potential then we might have paradise of artful bliss rather than imbalance of rage bait and nihilism capturing all our attention to the point of exhaustion.

I will wear more flowers in my hair in honour of you.

Chapter Threads

Queerstiscity – a made-up term to express the necessity of queerness.

Anohni – a singer, songwriter and visual artist who came up with the band Antony and the Johnsons.

'Marsha Magic' – a special form of magic rooted in radical imagination coined by Tourmaline, a visual artist and author of *Marsha, The Joy and Defiance of Marsha P. Johnson*.

A woman – a woman who could be me?

dreich – Scottish word for grey wet weather.

Gay Liberation Monument – the first piece of public art dedicated to gay rights by artist George Segal, made in 1984. It was originally meant for New York City to recognise the 10th anniversary of the Stonewall uprising. But as the funding for its completion was never honoured, it was then placed within the grounds of Stanford University in California where it was brutally vandalised, then moved to Wisconsin and finally placed at its permanent home in New York City in 1991.

Lightning bolts in a crowd – the moment everyone feels the electricity of something in unison.

Gaia philosophy – in Greek mythology Gaia is goddess of earth. It was later a theory co-developed by the chemist James Lovelock and microbiologist Lynn Margulis in the 1970s as a way of explaining the synergistic qualities of all things living, including earth itself, by arguing that organisms co-evolve with their environment.

Snake Beat PART VI

Re-birth,
Re-form,
the sound of the re's
continues in a
cacophony in my mind.
The more I look
at the map of what the
indigenous
named their
island
JA-MAY-CAH.
Re-birth,
Re-form,
Re-birth,
Re-pair.

8

Mary Wollstonecraft

Novelist, historian, pioneering feminist

'The being cannot be termed rational or virtuous, who obeys any authority, but that of reason.'

Mary Wollstonecraft

Born: 27 April 1759, Spitalfields, London
Died: 10 September 1797, Somers Town, London
Sign: Taurus[1]
Pronouns: She / Her

A Sense Memory: The Mother in Motion

There I was, clutching my tummy with a 10-week-old foetus inside. I'd arranged to be in residence on a little but booming island, perfectly called Tierra Bomba, off the coast of Cartagena, Northern Colombia (where I read the tarot, a story told in the letter to Pamela, p. 31), and I was on my way to spend some time writing and DJing in exchange for my digs. I'd arranged to do a sunset DJ set to a fabulous, glitzy and queer crowd around the pool, at a special place with a focus on sustainability, the arts and providing work structured on evolving eco-tourism. I knew I was wildly lucky and I was grateful to the point of a type of dumbstruck-ness that I spot in those of us who didn't ever prepare ourselves when they were growing up for their dreams coming true. When I'd arranged the gig, I'd had no idea I was going to be pregnant and that by proxy I'd be be politely declining the mouthwatering sorrel-toned rum cocktail offered to me on arrival in favour of a fresh watermelon juice instead. When I arranged this, I had no idea I'd have been spotting for a few days, and quite so slow on my feet.

Despite being reassured by a doctor and three different scans that the little lion in my belly is fine and placed 'normally' and told that 'spotting is common', I'd already been surprised by how much slower I would be, and that the expanding in a sensitive zone of my body, where I'd had fibroid removal surgery just over a year before, would be so tender and plump. I'd had no idea that, though you're not 'supposed to show' until further down the line, I wouldn't be able to stop looking at my roundness already and feeling such relief at its expanse and protrusion. I'd had no idea I would feel quite so womanly, so warm and alive with ideas of care. That I would look at everyone, wanting them to know, to be extra light with their usual brittleness / rebuttal to the world around them, to embrace one another and rejoice for the beautiful magic of being a human, literally an extraordinary vessel so precious I wish I'd learned to adore and protect my body long before now. I had no idea. I wish I'd known how to sleep and restore and prioritise being in tune with nature above anything else. It turns out being 10 weeks pregnant makes you want to tell the world how in love you are with the wonder of it all and that, yes, you are tinged with nerves, and hope that everything will be OK, but that the most natural thing to do is to be in the sea, with a tiny lion, who they tell you will arrive in the heat of summer, and likely roaring.

Mary Wollstonecraft

To bloom in summer feels just perfect for you.
The Caribbean sea, I thought, you must bob in the Caribbean sea right now . . . Before you're earthside, I thought too.

Tierra Bomba, February 2024

Dear My Unborn Child,

I want sunshine and adventure for you, **Lion**, adventure in nurture and nature and a life full of soft rest, fruits, and potent, true, dance-filled, supported and celebrated love. You have transformed my intention for this residency, on a tropical island that knows the art of parties. I want now to strengthen my knowledge of living sustainably. As a mother in motion, ready to write and create, paint pictures with words that I hope you, one day, will draw hope from when being pulled in the directions of limitlessness and lostness. I hope you will say yes to adventure but stay grounded in the joy, comfort and protection I wish for you always. For I am always learning that it's in the beams of the sun, and being able to turn your phone off for an entire day and flow in momentum, it's in weather and surety of sunsets and -rises. It's in the autonomy of not feeling like you have to do what everyone else is doing if you don't feel like it. It's in respecting the notion of freedom and femininity, it's in bravery, it's in books, watermelon juice and places that empower our fellow people.

Lots & lots of love
Mum Xx

Radical Journey-ing

I'm not the only womxn to feel such connection to the secrets of adventure when considered from the feminist perspective. Womxn have documented their travels, and their calling for travel and experience, for a long time. It is, however, not surprising to me that the mainstream doesn't represent motherhood and travel combined. But I see a paradigm where it co-exists, even if it is paced at a more soulful tempo. In media we are presented a very linear construct of what 'leisure' is, and of the ways we're expected to travel and 'relax' as womxn; the realms of travel and leisure are ones where womxn who present as hyper-gorgeous are repeatedly reminded we must be cautious because of our so-called fragility. 'Pampering' and looking fabulous in swimwear is projected as our main recreational desire, when off-the-beaten-track adventure is advertised for the boys and 'tomboys'. Though my core has been navigated and strengthened when I learned to know who I really was and travel through time and in different parts of the world. For it's our very own modern culture, upon the depth of our foundations, that we live embodied and full lives. For what's the point of Mother Earth doing her damnedest to show you paradise, if all we do is repeat the patterns of sabotage?

Mary Wollstonecraft was a philosopher by trade. She was the author of the seminal feminist essay 'A Vindication of the Rights of Woman', published in 1792, and was also a deep and impassioned chronicler of the eighteenth century, who did not take no for an answer. Women in those times died easily, were disrespected and disregarded and were not brought up to write and publish thought. But Mary whipped her time and mind into going against the grain and used her intense thought and wanderlust to write and publish essays and letters of resistance, and to travel.

In 1795, having survived a suicide attempt, she decided to take her infant daughter Fanny in search of stolen treasure across Scandinavia. On that trip, she wrote letters in a travelogue that's still loved and referenced today. Her affair with American revolutionary Gilbert Imlay (Fanny's father) had recently broken down. But she remembered him telling her that a Norwegian captain had abandoned the valuable silver cargo of one of his ships, and after Imlay suddenly broke off his relationship with Mary and said that he wanted nothing to do with raising their baby daughter, Mary vowed – in a bid for self-worth and brilliance – to hunt down this silver.

Letters Written in Sweden, Norway, and Denmark was the book that she birthed on that journey, despite being abandoned by Imlay (he was already living with another woman by the time she returned from her travels). On her voyage she suddenly came face to face with a peace she had never felt. She was inspired by the sublime scenery, and found herself in the ferality that saw her feeding her daughter wild strawberries.[2]

A Sense Memory: Meditations on motherhood and its becoming

I didn't know I wanted to become a mother until I did (and I think that was later than many others). I could, however, in my awe-sodden wade to identifying as a woman – not plain creature, kid, alien or black sheep – feel merciful stirrings inside me as I watched many of my beloveds become mothers. I realised that depending on where the news landed of a friend's pregnancy in my own menstrual cycle, it affected my instant reaction to their announcement. Sometimes, for example, I found myself flushed with undefined tears and other times I was struck with a type of astonishment and as a result would put my pregnant friend on a pedestal. Another beautiful woman to be marvelled at, growing in orb form. WOW, these women were so strong, and as powerful as God, I thought. Meanwhile, I was hoping that they had all the support they needed to thrive in all they were becoming, to stay afloat as soon-to-be mothers, and I vowed to try and 'show up', even if clumsily, even if far away. I'd be overcome with pride for my friends who cut the cords of troubled childhoods by defiantly renewing all that they'd experienced into something so profoundly beautiful.

Wollstonecraft was inspired by the Scottish Enlightenment (a movement I have only felt beckon me, from beyond the graves in which it's buried in the light through the stained glass in certain parts of Glasgow and the rosy view in which it's often viewed here in Scotland). But the enlightenment – when you take away the evangelicalism that surrounds its history in the advancement of sciences, industrialism and empire, and realise its problematic links with the upholding of only men and links to the transatlantic slave trade – reduces my enticement to the idea of being 'enlightened' to an interest in the language of radical boldness only. The Scots were not holding back on thinking big, marking a shift from the paradigm of religion to that of reason / sciences / philosophy. Improving society with these studies was central to the movement.

I am intrigued as to how that affected the women.

Wollstonecraft railed against the fashion of girls and young women, and the fact that women were told to concentrate on their looks:

> Taught from their infancy that beauty is woman's sceptre, the mind shapes itself to the body, and, roaming round its gilt cage, only seeks to adorn its prison.
>
> Mary Wollstonecraft

Wollstonecraft often chose to present herself ambiguously, and in plain-coloured cotton, choosing practicality and losing the frills sported by many women at the time. Simplicity in fashion became a feminist weapon of choice, which is so interesting to me in its contrast to the regalia, the swagger and the sparkle we find in other descriptions of the Sisterhood's clothes. Wollstonecraft's symbols were of a more quiet, sartorial kind.

Mary stood up again and again for the rights and freedom of women and yet, today, it's often her famous novel-writing daughter, Mary Shelley, who is better remembered. It was her strident and smart mother, though, who laid the foundation of greatness for her.

At 33, Wollstonecraft moved to the centre of Paris to experience the fervour of the French Revolution, which had taken place just three years before, in 1789. Demands for women's equality had been part of the fire that fuelled the revolution, and one of the key moments of the revolution had been the Women's March on Versailles in October 1789. The Women's Rights Movement was swelling with hope. The women at the heart of the movement – campaigning in the written word, coming together for conventions, storming important places – knew themselves as equals, and all this was happening in Paris, a meeting ground for like-minded thinkers from all over Europe. To practise revolution, we must live it.

Mary was in Paris in the winter of 1794–5, when things got even tougher. It was one of the coldest winters in hundreds of years. The Seine froze over, times were hard, and Mary was English, which made her unsafe in Paris while the French fought the British. She'd also just had a baby, and the father had left her.

More than four decades separated their time there, but I like to think of Mary Wollstonecraft and Jeanne Duval's spirits passing each other in the same streets they walked down in Paris. I imagine their time-travelling selves finding each other on the bank of the Seine, with horses galloping by, and people from all over the world being pulled around in carriages. The sounds of hoofs. The sounds of revolutionary words of courage being whispered in ornate Parisian courtyards: Mary just after the 1789 revolution, Jeanne in the heat of the 1848 revolution.

Mary was a staunch, unapologetic, intense campaigner and lover, unafraid of ruffling the feathers of any powerful male counterpart. For all the hardships she suffered, as a feminist, thinker and writer, she was one of the lucky ones, as far as the Sisterhood goes. There are countless works about her, which you can't say about all the other brave, globe-searching sistxrs, such as Pamela Colman Smith, Mary Seacole and Una Marson, not to mention Jeanne Duval. It's *really* hard not to notice that all of them – unlike Mary – were women of colour.

Why do we disassociate from the survival stories of Black women? Why is the societal response different? I want to hold us up as equals, as a tribe of women who must come together to repair the mess we're in. I'd be at the table with all these women, learning from them all, re-writing the manifestos just as Wollstonecraft rewrote gender rights against the prevailing traditions. For if Wollstonecraft was begging for the elite to consider devising better-suited paradigms for equal rights in the 1700s, I argue with complete conviction that we should be demanding this of our world right now. Fuck tradition if it hurts us. Create new ones that keep us all safe, like Marsha and Sylvia did. It is up to us to meld, recreate balance and write something new.

A Sense Memory: No mountain too high

I met my love 300 feet up in a mountain village on the south-easterly part of the motherland. I think I knew I loved him from the first moment I met him. I had been in an old and falling-apart Toyota, stuck to the leather back seat and driving upwards for nearly eight hours, as I'd managed to persuade a friend to take on a wild travel fantasy I'd had years previously to end a big adventure in Malawi. This particular part of the itinerary meant travelling to a village so high up it was legendarily difficult to get to, but once you were there, you could regroup from the tough journey there at an eco-lodge called The Mushroom Farm, which had a permaculture garden and was completely off-grid. It had floated inconspicuously online // a positive algorithm, a recommendation from a dear friend in a Facebook message 'If you ever go back to Malawi, you MUST check out this place' she'd written.

Visiting parts of Africa, I've felt a feeling that can't be described in the English language, beyond a colonial form of intellectualism. For the continent offers a heart-led and felt experience that's way off the track of the luxury that capitalism lures us to beat, as though travelling is a board game for the elite. In juxtaposition, the vastness and ancient richness of the African countries I've visited cannot be reduced in any gloss of European dominance or understanding. There I was, having travelled for hours, in search of this place I'd seen online called the Mushroom Farm and knew nothing about beyond stunning photos of earthen structures, promises of **permaculture** and views to blow minds. It was quite scary, being so high and physically bumping over the soil as we drove off-road past forest fires. When we finally tumbled out at the destination, I remember looking at my feet, squished into a pair of sliders, so covered in dried earth that

I had no idea what they looked like before they were transformed to red clay. But I felt pulled to this place, and I was reconciling with having persuaded my friend to come this far from anything we could familiarise ourselves with. The minute we got out of the car, three medium-sized cartoon-style dogs began barking at us relentlessly and the delirium had me bypassing my usual apprehension of dogs.

'Oh, Cameron will be down in a minute,' said a giggly man I later learned was called Bishop. I ordered a beer and wondered if I'd actually died enroute, because this place seemed too surreal. We were far up in the mountains and fairy lights hung over a breathtaking campsite more than 2,000 feet above sea level and wooden structures guided us to more areas of wonder. I wasn't believing my eyes, and then he arrived, a very handsome human with eyes that stopped all thought except for that I had somehow always known him. Which was ludicrous, as he'd been living in a treehouse for years up here, on a mountain top in Northern Malawi. But my instinct had been right. I was supposed to visit the place, I was supposed to meet this person and I'm thankful all the time that he showed me that dreaming for an oasis in nature bound with community, time and beauty can in fact come true.

It's all been done before. The world, travelled over and in and through. A cosmos of experience is what we float in under stars that make us relatively and wondrously small.

A fate too tragic

In 1797 Mary Wollstonecraft – one of two members of this Sisterhood who gave birth – died while giving birth to her second daughter, Mary Shelley. At that time one in approximately every 100 to 150 births resulted in maternal death. One hundred and eighty-two years later, in 1979, Grace Jones gave birth to her son. Although modern medicine has greatly improved maternal outcomes, it doesn't mean childbirth is equally safe for all women. In the UK today, Black women are still nearly three times more likely to die in childbirth than white women.[3] It frightens me to stay caught in the statistics, especially as I transition into the multiplicity that is ongoing motherhood. How do I outstretch my arms, my womb, my heart, and re-wire it all? Start again? Create safety for women everywhere?

I can imagine it and in my prayer I imagine:

Rowan trees planted the doorways of each one of our homes

Twigs of **birch** to make each of our cradles

and

imagine that a mother as strong as Earth holds all the lessons in which we need, these thoughts of nature spells grant me hope for the present still living and all that's yet to be birthed.

August 2024

Scotland

Dear Mary

I'm so intrigued to ask you about your inspiration found in the Scottish Enlightenment? Were some of the guys as pompous as I imagine?

In your work, you commented on the woman's association with our own image. What do you think about weight loss medicine? What do you think about plastic surgery? Botox? Gendered advertising of unachievable beauty standards and our anxieties being soothed by 'Mummy's glass of wine'?

I'm also intrigued to ask you? When weaving and re-weaving the fabric and grounds of our individual morals? Did any trips blow you away enough to think something completely different than you did before it?

I feel so many men treated you badly in your life. How did you find it in your heart to keep loving? With all that you know, would you have done things differently?

I hope you don't mind me asking, but I know you attempted death by suicide in your life, I'm so sorry that you felt you wanted life to end. Was it the disappointment of the romantic relationships, as suggested in history books or was it a want for the escape of how painful all trauma can be? These days, there is a world of modalities and therapies out there that alleviate some of the hurt; you wouldn't even be able to imagine how complex and brilliant modes of support can do the miracle work of redemption, recovery, reconciliation and change. It may sound mad, but sometimes I wish for everyone to be given the chance and access to a life they love that results in so much more kindness than there is.

Your Mary went on to thrill the world with her writing; you would be so proud. Perhaps you know this already and you watched over her, as I feel my lost loved ones (or even those with whom I had complicated relationships, when they were alive) guide me in ghostly luminous love.

Thank you for all your words and work and spirit. Mary, I can only wish that you know how much it has inspired so many.

Chapter Thread

Lion – The nickname I gave my bump while pregnant with my first child.

permaculture – a harmonious integration of landscape that provides people with food, energy and shelter without damaging the environment.

rowan trees – in Celtic and Norse tradition, the rowan tree is a 'tree of life' that they say, if planted at your door, will protect homes from harm.

birch – birch trees are mythologically associated with purification and renewal.

Snake Beat PART VII

Reeeeeesponsibilty
comes up in the
rhythm of the
Rasta beat poets
who spend and
have spent lives
creating new
pathways
I thank my elders and
feel so lucky to be
alive now but the r's
don't quieten
down.
Re-birth,
Re-form,
Re-birth,
Re-form.

9

Nanny of the Maroons

Leader of the rebellion for the emancipation of enslaved people in Jamaica

Out Of Many, One People

A Jamaican phrase on the brilliance of unity

Born: 1686, Ghana
Died: 1733, Jamaica
Sign: Unknown
Pronouns: She / Her

Nanny of the Maroons[1] is an awe-inspiring figure in Jamaican history, whose legendary exploits have left an indelible mark on the fight against British rule in the eighteenth century.

Born in Ghana and brought to Jamaica to be part of the **Transatlantic slave trade**, it is argued that she either ran away from capture or was never even enslaved at all. Nanny showed extraordinary leadership skills and profound knowledge of guerrilla warfare. Her life was so bold and full of spirit that it feels like it could have come from folklore. Nanny escaped enslavement at a young age and fled to the lush Eastern Mountains of Jamaica, known as the Portland region today. These mountains were where rebels, freedom fighters and runaways hid and fought the British Army for years. Nanny would eventually become one of their leaders. When I say Nanny was formidable, I'm not saying it lightly. Over the course of 50 years, she led more than 800 African people out of enslavement to freedom. She did all this in the eighteenth century – but there is no end to the lessons we can still learn from her about opposing oppressive systems.

Originally from the Ashanti tribe, Nanny held the wisdom of West African spirituality inside her. She put in place ingenious techniques to protect the other escaped slaves in the Jamaican mountains – including putting a huge cauldron in place at the foot of the trail that led to her encampment, known as Nanny Town. Curious enemies would sometimes stop to smell the fumes from the boiling cauldron. The fumes were designed to make them either pass out, or tempt them so much that they would fall into the cauldron.

'You cannot mess with a Maroon; we are a unique and proud people who have immense power when needed,' my guide explained as I set out to visit the legendary Nanny Falls, in Maroon Town. I decided to trek out there on a solo pilgrimage one afternoon on my first trip to Jamaica. I was in real need of drastic healing to lift my consciousness and heavy heart. I was low, I needed soothing surroundings to remind me that I came from somewhere beautiful and that heartbreak happens to those who choose to give in to the feeling of potential and vulnerability when we open ourselves to love in its wholeness. There was no place more healing to me at that moment than Nanny Falls: the same waterfalls Nanny is thought to have taken wounded soldiers to in order to revive them. Legend has it that the soldiers' battle scars and injuries would disappear like magic when cleansed in these waters, and that if their bruises and cuts didn't heal from the waters, they wouldn't be sent back out to fight until they had fully recovered.

I felt so moved to be there; there really was magic everywhere. 'We have passed on our knowledge of herbs, plants and African wisdom and communicate with the plants,' Deano, founder of Falls Tours, said to me when I interviewed him about the sacred nature of the site. Folklore is predominantly told orally and passed on in the style of myth, legend and fairy tale.

I'm drawn to the properties of the **cacoon vine** that can be found deep in the vegetation of the Maroon Hills. It was used to make crowns that soldiers wore on their heads, in the style of stealthy regal warriors.

Heritage: MIXED

I am from a mixed background, and the idea of categorising class or heritage in box-ticking exercises has tired me out. In the years that I've grown up, the world has become even more siloed, and the need for quick and condensed explanations has become asked for more and more. My mother-line is nearly completely Scottish with some Irish mixed in. There is a mixture of tailors, golfers, engineers, teachers and if you were to go back far enough, my name, Cairney, they say, comes from Celtic warriors and noble folk in the **Bronze Age**, who were buried under mounds of rocks called cairns, in honour of the transition to the afterlife through the lands. Over thousands of years much of this Celtic tradition was erased by English colonisers during the Highland Clearances (all in all between 1750 and 1860), which obliterated any clan life.

My father-line is Jamaican. Facts about this side of my bloodline have been swallowed up by the displacement and migration of my people over centuries. How many secrets about my past are there on the seabed from the transatlantic trade of humans? Through modern technology, I've even managed to trace my DNA as far away and as unexpectedly as the Balkans and across the sea to regions of West Africa and beyond. My biological father's mother is still alive. She is over 90: a pastor who's lived a life of unrelenting faith and is a figure of undeniable care for many in her community. My dad, her son, did not escape the generational trauma of my grandmother's generation being uprooted from Jamaica to what – at least in theory – was going to be the welcoming Britain where he would end up being born. This dad passed away when I was nineteen. I hadn't seen him since I was three. But I have been reunited with extended family; this all on occasion staggers me and on other occasions has me counting every star for how blessed I feel to be held and protected by so much familial love from chosen family and those with whom I share a bloodline.

I recognise my face in Jamaicans. I hear my heartbeat in the fuzz of dub and a call back to nature in the subversion of Rastafarianism.[2] Both lines are like traces on maps coded with routes to personal sacred understanding. Like many, I am forced to look backwards in order to configure myself, but without much archive and with a lot of grief to unpick and work through. Sometimes I feel like I know all I need to about myself and just let myself settle down into an ambiguous understanding of my identity: an immaterial definition guided by a determination to create pride in all of us with mixed backgrounds, regardless of our difference, contrasts or any conflicts and tension. I've known this to come with an openness that propels me beyond any formed rigidities in nationalism.

> We are all VITALISED souls that many of those in our lineage before us, laid a path for in their survival and these paths lead us all over the world, every single one of us.

My ancestors' island is one of the most bountiful and bombastic places in the Caribbean. Jamaica today is rich in multicultural reference, legend and infectious vitality. Vitality means to be energised, enthusiastic and so alive that one's nature sings. Vibrancy makes Jamaica one of the most remarkable islands on the earth. A notable vitality that rushes through my blood like fyah burns bright in the darkest of hours.

When I asked my aunt on my father's side if she was up for filling in some gaps of my family tree, a few days later my phone became a root in my hand, as my eyes grew so did my heart when I saw the faces in the old photographs she sent back. 'This is your great grandad,' she wrote. He was a farmer in Spanish Town. In my hand was an image of the most erudite farmer I've ever seen. Sleekly ironed creases in his linen marl grey trousers, held up with a matching leather belt, a white shirt tucked in and a flat cap. His cheekbones, pronounced like mine when I have time for exercise, and a glint in his eye, that binds us as blood-related even through a picture and all these years later.

A Sense Memory: Land Yearning

I once bought an acre of land at auction without seeing it, because I so desperately wanted my free time to be spent naked and jumping into the river that ran at its edge. I loved the idea of returning to a place that took the edge off limitless choices, to offer space for my community made up of friends and other folk who feel charged by growing plants and constructing sustainable daily lives. I spoke with radical horticulturalists and learned about the migration of unwanted roots and the survival of hardy trees that thrive by water. 'Deluded,' some said; 'interesting' said others, while I giddily relayed the experience of buying land at auction. It was thrilling. It felt like reparations for my very cells.

> I've always said to my men friends, If you really care for me, darling, you will give me territory. Give me land, give me land.
>
> Eartha Kitt[3]

Nanny's military prowess was unparalleled. She lead the Windward Maroons, a community of escaped people that grew in numbers over decades and happened via organised mission, including raids of plantations, freeing as many people as possible. The Maroons established their own self-governing settlements in the rugged and impenetrable (for many) regions of Jamaica, where Nanny fearlessly spearheaded the fight for freedom. Her strategic brilliance and ability to unite disparate Maroon factions were instrumental in their successful defence against British forces.

She used any tactic she could to outsmart the British again and again: ambush, guerrilla warfare, camouflage utilising locally grown foliage. Her spirit and unwavering determination for justice inspired her people, instilling in them a sense of unity and resilience that propelled the Maroons forward.

The idea of Nanny defying forced servitude and risking her life somehow gives me strength when I'm tired and feel like an imposter, and when at points I actually *know* that I'm rightly alienated from systems that pointedly don't humanise me . . . I'm still a citizen of the global majority who knows how to survive and thrive regardless of the fatiguing rise of the far right. She kept on going, with purpose, creating fruitful lives for folk creating new identities during the times of slavery. If she can do that, we can all find our sense of purpose now.

Nanny's influence extended far beyond the battlefield. She was revered as a spiritual leader and believed to possess supernatural powers that guided and protected her people. Her wisdom, courage, and unyielding spirit continue to inspire generations, making her an enduring symbol of resistance, freedom, and empowerment.

Quilting community

They say 'it takes a village' and it likely does. Not only to bring up children, but to look after one another as adults in wholeness and multilayers, to accept the nuances and ebb and flow of our collective patchwork quilts called life. A small square for when someone once hurt us, another for our solemn whispers of healing and prayer, another for knowing what our contentment can be, another for mundanity, for the satisfaction of doing laundry, for our affection for all that's living . . . pets, plants, a tree we see every day, for our shiver at a memory of an injury, for our gut-excitement at stumbling upon our favourite pop song, for the realistic order and chaos and back to order again, then the unexpected again. A square for an emotional breakthrough when you realise a heart may be stitched up and fixed again, a patch for when a stranger smiles back at you, a thread of forgiveness for something you regret as you move forward, a heart shape for the joy of plans coming together, for communal eating and merrymaking. A patchwork of everyday life draped around our shoulders like armour, a truth of a sense of community that defies the convention of imposed family and creates a blend of love within a group, that pings and resonates between clusters of streets in neighbourhoods everywhere. A section of honour and thanks for our ancestors, because really, it takes a tribe for us all to feel safe and happy.

Similarly to Sister Jeanne's story in The Immortal Sisterhood (p. 87), much of what we know about Nanny's life comes from oral storytelling traditions and folklore, proving that even with limited historical records, her impact on Jamaican history and her status as a legendary figure cannot be overstated. Nanny of the Maroons stands as a testament to the indomitable spirit of those who fought against depravity and serves as a reminder of the power of unity and resilience in the face of adversity. Because some things are worth organising for.

You can find a picture of Nanny on the current Jamaican $500 banknote.

In October of 1975, Nanny was added to Jamaica's list of National Heroes, the only one who is a woman. She is celebrated on National Heroes Day in Moor Town, which lands on the third Monday of every October. Celebrations include invoking spirit by drinking spirits and dancing to the playing of the **Abeng**.

Dear Nanny

I wanted to tell you about when I visited the town of San Basilio de Palenque, Colombia – founded by Benkos Biohó, a West African leader who created the first freed town of the Americas, formed in 1603, where over years an agreement was signed to let the people of the town remain in liberty, by official decree, from the Spanish crown that had colonised it. It took until 2005 to become officially recognised as a masterpiece of the Oral and Intangible Heritage of Humanity. This remarkable visit held a distinct and unique value to me. It encompassed the taste of freedom, the language of freedom, the medicine of freedom, the organisation of freedom and how music and even hair's importance is threaded through all of it.

Having arrived via various modes of public transport, including train, a glitter-burnished bus and jumping on the back of a motorbike, I ended up racing through the streets of Palenque, and for the first time I was able to behold an imagining that can be encased in a pain. This imagining transformed the truth that slavery is a part of my ancestry to a place of emancipation. The air that day gave it to me. Happy spirits of liberation, shook ground when I heard the drums played and a mutual love of music felt ecstatically in my DNA when I walked around and huge speakers bellowed afrobeats. It is a wonderful place, one that offered a poignant respect for its origins but also felt like a modern town I would come across somewhere in the motherland. I was honoured to pay to get my hair braided in my peaceful gratitude to my African ancestors for their ingenuity and wisdom. Because in the 1500s hair-braiding was used as a way of creating encrypted maps for the enslaved. Women had learned to style cornrowed afro hair into the shape of literal routes to safety, with the lines and shapes on the braided person's scalp secretly offering directions to the refuge that was Palenque. It reminded me of the work that must have been inherent to all the coming together and all the organisation necessary for resisting what were deplorable conditions for so many. I know that you were from different tribes and regions and were displaced from family members and that Africa has never been a monolith, despite the West's attempts to simplify and homogenise it. Any pushing back that was done in those times would've required such amounts of energy and patience in communication beyond spoken language and an enduring sharing of knowledge that words do not suffice to do justice.

& I'm unsure that a thank you does either, so I will leave this letter unended and with a promise of commitment to everyone being free.

Gemma
Xx

Chapter Threads

Transatlantic slave trade – overall 400 years of forced labour across the United States of America, the Caribbean and South America. It involved immense violence and in Jamaica alone, one million African people were enslaved for the import of goods, mostly sugar and coffee, to the UK and Europe.

cacoon vine – a huge cacoon-shaped climber with big seed pods, otherwise known as African Dream Herb.

The Bronze Age – c.2500–700 BCE, The Bronze Age in Britain is named due to the advancement of tools in these times from stone to bronze, which marked other advancements in human life including the invention of early writing systems.

Abeng Horn – a cattle horn played by the maroons as a wind instrument to communicate to troops and plantation escapees across mountainous terrain.

Snake Beat PART VIII

I think of the
symbolism of what
we know to be
royal, the British
Empire, the
celebration of
castles and a
crown.
Re-birth
Re-form
I think of the storm
and lightning
bolts that I watched
bounce off of the
English Channel
outside my
bedroom
window the
night the British
press
clambered to
get a picture of
another
royal
baby
Re-birth.

10

Mary Seacole

Healer, doctor, herbalist, staunch advocate for democratising access to healthcare

'Time is a great restorer, and changes surely the greatest sorrow into pleasing memory.'

Mary Seacole, *Wonderful Adventures of Mrs. Seacole in Many Lands*, 1857

Born: 23 November 1805, Kingston, Jamaica
Died: 14 May 1881, Paddington, London, England
Sign: Sagittarius
Pronouns: She / Her

Mary Seacole's mother – whom records refer to only as Mrs Grant – was not enslaved. Born in Kingston, Jamaica, of Creole descent through her mother's line, Mrs Grant was of African and European heritage. Mary's father – James Grant – was of Scottish lineage, a military man stationed on the island under British imperial instruction. From the limited research available, Mary did not have a defining relationship with her father during her childhood. By contrast, she was heavily influenced by her mother. Mrs Grant was a hospitality business marvel, an owner of a reputable lodging house on the island, called Blundell Hall. A surge of land ownership of formerly enslaved people was common around the time, and Mary as a child would've been brought up with her mother tending a vegetable patch, her skills clearly thriving in growing food and medicinal herbs.

Word clearly spread far and wide about Mrs Grant's establishment. In 1874, Godfrey Turner, a special correspondent for the *Daily Telegraph*, wrote in *Geographical Magazine*:

> Blundell Hall is the place for . . . salt fish & ackee the fish being Newfoundland Cod, which is also the cheapest food among the ~~negro~~ labouring class and the ackee being a useful fruit which was brought into Jamaica during slave time and is not very unlike a hard-boiled egg in appearance and flavour.

It seems *The Telegraph* has long been printing reductive news. Spending her formative years in Blundell Hall, Mary must have formed a deep sense of movement and travel through the people who came to stay there, as evidenced in her later voyages and expeditions. It's here that Mary would wake to the sounds of bells[1] from the local church and the bugle. Kingston at this time would have been alive with a rich and inspiring sonic palette.

The Doctress

As well as running Blundell Hall, Mrs Grant was also a renowned and resolute healer, known by many as 'The Doctress', a name she came to be fondly remembered by. It's telling that Mary Seacole – the almighty life saver of so many – is also known as 'The Doctress' in the same way her mother was. Florence Nightingale, the nurse and Mary's contemporary, whose work had a similar effect to Mary's, was nicknamed 'The Wild Swan'. Unlike her white contemporary, though, Mary didn't have her remarkable skills as a nurse recognised during her lifetime. Esteemed medical circles worldwide would not even allow her to hold the title of nurse without her proving layer after layer of skill and knowledge. She knew all too well that this was because of the shade of her skin.

Her mother's influence led Mary to study herbalism. She displayed scientific agility by combining familial knowledge with local knowledge, and then adding this to the medicinal traditions of other countries, and used her dolls to practice on: 'whatever disease was most prevalent in Kingston, be sure my poor doll soon contracted it', she noted in her autobiography.

As a teenager, Mary single-handedly chose solo adventure. She travelled to England more than once, eagerly studying European medicine, to complement the herbalism in which she excelled, but also enduring constant racism. Undeterred, she continued to travel; in 1825 she travelled alone to the Bahamas, Haiti and Cuba, where she bought and foraged for special herbs and spices to make preserves, jams and pickles to sell.

A Sense Memory: I have never been drawn to the weapons displayed in museums of old stuff

In certain regions of Jamaica today, I've noted how the past can sear into the present. How references can jump and hop from place to place, as I write from my newfound homeland – Scotland. There are many reminders of Scotland's particular (and not often talked about) involvement in the Transatlantic slave trade and in the British Empire's retch-worthy rule of forced labour and displacement; where the financial riches acquired by the sweat and blood of the cruelly enslaved were originally hoarded on shores on the West African coast, far from Jamaica. Evidence of Scotland's incursion into Jamaica persists in so many parts of both countries today: words, surnames, songs . . . **scotch bonnets**.

Shivers surge as I study the map of the island of Jamaica, an imprinted geological shape on my heart. I often have visions of the familiar terrain of the Blue Mountains, endless waterfalls and dilapidated structures of worship, so many places mirroring the map of the UK . . . and I imagine the land trodden by those of whom I am a humble descendant. But there's a dot to dot of displacement, depending on where you land in the timeline, and a past so many would choose to erase. A geographer I am not, but my sense memory, my DNA, responds and shakes to the map markings as I learn the geography of my ancestors' island, Jamaica. Further studying the map, I see more evidence of Scotland's violent past: a disused ruin called 'Edinburgh Castle', which sits atop a hill a few miles east from a town called Inverness. English violence is marked, too: Devon, Penzance, Windsor, are all a stone's throw from places on the island where my Jamaican ancestors were born. Back in my home city of Edinburgh, I walk past Jamaica Street. I don't want to think about why a street in a Scottish city is named after the island. But if Scotland built streets named after the territories it claimed then . . . Jamaica gained independence from the British in 1962.

It's hard to imagine that in 1805 in the Caribbean, if you weren't born white, you were likely bound by the atrocity and the unnaturalness of enslavement. In contemporary times of distracting capitalism, sometimes I feel a low buzz of guilt about the society I was born into. I have a choice about where I live and how, which many of my ancestors did not. I try to hold my head high in the fog, I seek restorative justice and care radically in a search for tenderness and restoration while looking forward, knowing that I'm free; and I mourn those before me. Having invested time getting to know the Caribbean, I see where some pain has been transmuted into action and the carving out of some of the most inspiring and alchemising art, thought and island specific identities. No one can tell me that some of the best food and music in the whole world doesn't come from Jamaica, for example.

> The only cure will be a transformation of the whole society and an entirely new knowledge order altogether otherwise we will remain trapped in this. It is through language that you and I are able to now talk with each other, develop a mechanism to understand one another, do you see the immense potential there?! Language is entirely the point!
>
> Sylvia Wynter, Jamaican Writer and Philosopher on transformation from Offshoot Interview with Bedour Alagraa[2]

During a stay in Kingston in 1836, Mary met and married Edwin Seacole, a white British sea merchant. Sadly, a long and happy marriage was not to be: Edwin's health was poor, and despite Mary's close care he died, aged 41, in 1844. She dealt with her grief by working harder than ever, helping treat Jamaicans afflicted by an outbreak of cholera, and later in a similarly epidemic-hit Panama.

Mary was taught the West African traditions of her mother, whose healing techniques had passed on through the generations – taught orally with precision and faith. Mary treated myriad ailments, illnesses and wounds without reliance on Western infrastructure. Using herbs and earth-grown medicine, she also expanded and fused the medicinal approaches she had learned from peers around the world, including European, Central American and Indigenous practices. In her 75 years she proved to be a master of healing and was driven by a desire to take care of others. Her extraordinary ability to heal and bestow her gifts on others leaves me with lasting, tangible pearls of admiration. So many of us have remarkable gifts but are too afraid of their power and the commitment and honing they require to use them to their full effect. Mary taught me that acts of service create sustainability, and how nature can heal our bodies and improve the economy of marginalised communities. In times where racialised bodies can be so readily pathologised, frameworks of care from our own elders and the natural world can harness our sense of connection and deservedness to well-being – and that excites me beyond belief. Today there are long-term goals among researchers and campaigners to use the medicinal benefits of local Jamaican plants to create a profitable and sustainable herbal industry that will empower and mobilise generations to come. I, for one, can feel Mary's influence at work here.

When the Crimean War broke out in 1853, Mary went to England again, offering her services to the British army, but was rejected despite impeccable references from senior officials. Not one to give up, she raised money to get to Crimea, where she set up 'The British Hotel', a restaurant and shop, where she fed and nursed hundreds of British soldiers. Her embodied innovation proved not only life-saving for so many, but tells a potent tale about one person's capacity for courage in crisis that we can all learn from. Undeterred by battle, she would regularly take her horse to the front lines of the Crimean War to offer sandwiches and bandages to fighting soldiers.

Peace following the Crimean War sadly meant The British Hotel was no longer needed, and Mary went bankrupt. Ever enterprising, Seacole wrote her own story, in her published autobiography, *Wonderful Adventures of Mrs. Seacole in Many Lands*, and was credited as being the first Black woman to have written and published an autobiography. She documented her story on her terms and did so unapologetically.

When I analyse the common ways in which history has been documented and how it's so often taught in Western society, I feel a desperate urge to try and find new forms through which we can experience *all* the stories that are out there. What about the stories – the infinite stories – that don't exist in history books or biographies or official accounts? If Mary had not written and published her autobiography, how much would we have known from her perspective? How much would our image of her have been left to the memories of people who almost certainly saw her as belonging to a lesser class?

This – critically – still applies all these years later. If I do not explore and uncover the source of what I choose to consume – like where a coffee bean was grown or who has edited what I'm ingesting (this applies to film and literature too) – if I do not think about who commissioned, designed, wrote and created the end result of something, my access to the truth is going to remain murky and diluted. Think of all the biopics of great women that have been made. So many of them tell their stories through the eyes of others. How many of them were made by men? How many of those men were privately educated?

> Inside the word 'emergency' is 'emerge'; from an emergency, new things come forth. The old certainties are crumbling fast. But danger and possibilities are sisters,
>
> Rebecca Solnit, *Hope in the Dark: The Untold History of People Power*

When honouring Mary, it feels important to take heed of the mixture of luck and strength she needed to reject the norms of the times she lived in – especially in a country so heavily enslaved by the British. The empire was in full bloom at the time and the dehumanisation of those racialised as non-white had long been conditioned and normalised among those reaping slavery's vast financial benefits. How did Mary and her mother cultivate such resistance while in the Caribbean? Was it through the care and hospitality that they dedicated their lives to? Was it their gifts for healing and willingness to heal all, come what may? Was it because their excellence was so necessary to many? Perhaps it was something to do with their connection and deep faith in the power of nature, and how they relied on it to guide their healing. I trace many of the blessings in my life back to the glory of nature.

I try to learn from Mary and Mrs Grant's focus and tenacity. I've found that even a simple act of kindness can be profound when the time and energy you're devoting to it is in service of something or someone beyond yourself. Their choices lead me to wonder about womxn today and our own choices: when choosing our careers in modern times, does our so-called maternal instinct guide us towards jobs of care? And is that instinct exploited for the benefits of capitalism? Somehow, Mary found a way to use her caring abilities on her own terms, and that is a lesson I carry with me.

Sister Synchronicity: EARTH

Sarsaparilla, soursop and ceresee, herbs plugging me back to health to create iron and reduce inflammation, minerals engineering my remarkable vessel of a body asking to move through life with vitality. I sip slowly and don't think twice about the flavour of earth, with a knowingness that I become akin to soil in the aroma and taste.

I bound my right leg in warm comfrey leaves when I slipped in the rain and broke it in three places while hiking up a steep Scottish hill, to encourage the bone to grow back together.

I anoint my hands in **between my thumb and forefinger** with oils, bergamot and ylang ylang, to ground any restlessness. I reach for the freshness of eucalyptus when I want to remember the importance of exhalation with intent.

I spend my savings on massage and acupuncture, and dream of my own garden full of purple, both the spikes of gorse and its eruption of deep yellow flower in spring, and trumpet trees known in Jamaica, for they upturn their leaves, to reveal a shade of silver when thunder is coming. Adventure in treatments, travel, exertion and super-nature are all part of my evolving affinity.

I'm sense-aware of the unpredictable climate I live in. I've learned to flow with temperature-play and wax lyrical about the necessity I feel for a sauna that I can sweat in every other day.

I'm so proud to be Jamaican; it's in the words, it's **magical realism** that is embedded in the multiplicity of our culture, it's in the natural bodies of water. We have hundreds of waterfalls, where myth streams in splattering water, we have dancing, silver schools of tropical fish that leap from the sea if you spend enough time staring at the turquoises of a day at any land edge.

ROOTS

Mary's refusal to abide by the terms of the time she lived in is both an inspiration and a challenge to me. It was a radical act to forge the life she wanted: it was nothing short of revolutionary.

The thoughts of the slow violence swell at the root of my sacrum // spine. I remind myself that my history goes even further back, and that Jamaica was a land before empire and the start of the transatlantic slave trade. The indigenous people of **Xaymaca** were the Redware and Taíno tribes. I feel a sense of belonging beyond servitude: pride. It's a pride that extends to Mary and her mother. What they achieved despite the times they lived in. We as a people must know Mary Seacole's story and take time to study herbs and fauna – in the demise of access to free healthcare in the UK, supplementing and preventing disease with ancestral knowledge is intrinsic to our route back to belonging inside of our bodies and on a planet where elements of health can be achieved in our connection to the plants and natural landscape around us.

Our other Mary interconnected in this literary offering of thanks is Mary Wollstonecraft, who tragically died during the birth of her universally well-known daughter, Mary Shelley, the author of *Frankenstein*. Childbirth was one of the most common causes of early death for women back then. It was a man's world: the state offered no in-depth research or facilities for the sake of reproductivity or women's health. It was left to other women to bring forth new life. For millennia midwives have been labelled witches, but it was they who saved lives through oral knowledge, tradition, and extensive medical knowledge; they were just never given the trust to define their skills as such. It will be a stain on history for ever that these women were treated so brutally and branded so viciously, when they were the exact people human-kind needed to survive and from whom we were able to learn about the deeply powerful symbiosis between nature and our bodies.

In Sister Audre's retelling of her family tree, in her book *Zami: A New Spelling of My Name*, she writes rhythmically about musical seas, and darts artfully between descriptions of island life in the Caribbean for her parents, and relates how her mother was born into the loving palms of her mother's sister Anni, as were her mother's six siblings. Audre writes of the unique powers and ways of the matriarchal Caribbean, describing a 'strengthening of the earth' by pouring rum directly onto it to grow food:

> I long to be such a woman of ground and water and to have that depth of apothecary knowledge, to be made up of the churning strength of islands close to the salty roars of ocean, even when up in the hills. Sometimes I feel like I know I am these island women of past.

Mary was not squeamish and in her autobiographies she describes the tumultuous, sometimes brutal nature of midwifery. How did she preserve her own mental and emotional health amid the extreme everyday suffering she witnessed and tended to?

The modern trope of the 'strong Black woman' is one that sits uncomfortably with me. It's not for us to wear the traumas of the world with ease just because the media can sometimes proclaim us as 'otherworldly' creatures apparently able to survive (or even enjoy) toiling for the benefits of those allowed beyond the glass ceiling and for the endeavours of big conglomerates.

It heartens me to know that Mary's work lives on so vividly in present-day Jamaica where she's on the curriculum as a recommended significant individual, despite not being a mandatory subject. My wonderings are how thorough the teaching of

Black history is in schools currently and its regarded importance. What are the emotional effects, from how it's taught, if taught at all? When surely truth, its complex triggers and discourse of accountability need expressing with a serious rigour and commitment. Plus the balance of sharing solutions found, rebellion organised and restorative repair against and despite deplorable human behaviour are the lessons I want to learn from.

Her own story, published in her words, was released in 1857. It defied the industry and sold more copies than anyone expected, and had to be printed in a second edition the following year. It came out in the same year as David Livingstone's *Missionary Travels and Researches in South Africa*, and Charles Baudelaire's poetry collection *Les Fleurs du Mal*. If only I had been able to give Jeanne Duval a copy of *Wonderful Adventures of Mrs. Seacole in Many Lands*, in its bright yellow jacket, to read instead!

January 2020

Dear Mary

I'm writing this from Jamaica, where we've brought back our dad for the first time since he left the island in 1962. I have such a (sacred) geometric family tree. It's sometimes exhausting to try to decipher how I feel about it all. In attempts to feel whole, I can find myself at points in a slightly contented reverie, floating . . . lightweight in a silken abyss of other realms that tie me to my island rather than overthinking the nuanced truth that I have two fathers. One who brought me up, one no longer alive, and both came from this paradise where I have schools of tropical fish dance for me, and let soursop coat the insides of my oesophagus with a melting of nervousness. I love it here. I wasn't in the best way when I first came, in fact I nearly didn't come, but my sister wouldn't let me back out when we had been planning this trip for so long. What was it like back then? Your one-woman mission to overcome the superiority you faced from many has created fortitude for us all. I would love to know more about your own self care, your very own framework of thriving? What company did you keep? We know in our cells and microbiome that it's herbs and our relationship to them that could enhance so much of our life but I've felt a spiral of mourning sometimes for how disconnected we are from the natural world. There's so much war, Mary. Were you able to find light in the wounding? How did it feel to watch people get better? Getting better has always felt wild to me, it's where a concept of care takes a new dimension, becomes enticing enough for one to fantasise about centring a life around it. Only to leave me a bit breathless as I realise it's a part of life that is most deep, most effective, when shared and that so much of life guards it away for the few. I wonder what you would make of the world right now. There are murmurings of a new flu breaking out in China, I think that news may be exaggerated, despite some of the internet likening it to the plague. Farfetched if you ask me.

I dreamed about you. You were more vivid than the sky out my window or secrets. I imagined you going about your day like this: 'The sway in her walk is in time with the pace of her considered and precise thoughts as she approaches the market. Mary has a list of what she wants, what is needed: she is here to pick up herbs and spices for healing broths and preserves. The pencil marks and swirls of her looped handwriting are definite and researched, clasped tightly in her palm on paper but almost vibrating. There are people everywhere, moving in the unison of live trade, hearts beating to a rhythm of organised bustle; her eyes are alight, for all the colours to move from her sight and into her brain. She thought to herself how even though the greys and muted dusty browns of the blouses and breeches from the settlers that came through Blundell Hall had an air of 'properness' to them, they were hell to keep spotless, even if she did adore the smell of the linen being cleaned, she associated dull clothing with drudgery. At this moment, she thinks of the enrichment she could feel when she saw these bodies on this island wrapped and held in such colour and precious embellishments of jewellery like she was seeing right now on her trip. One seller that particularly catches her eye has two different coloured eyes, one as hazel orange as the autumn landscapes her British friends had told her about in England

and the other glassy blue like the morning sea she'd travelled over to get to Haiti. His glistening unusual eyes are framed with golden wire wrapped crown-like around his head. She notices how healthy true beauty is. In all her studies she'd never come across an explanation for the health benefits of colourful material and precious metal and its display such as she was experiencing on this trip to Haiti. She buys dried sunflower leaves after he explains he lived in the mountains and that it was sometimes hard to get to a doctor, so his community often boiled them to drink if they had a cough. The conversation had been gloriously patchworked due to the barriers of mother tongue and broken French and English, but she had enjoyed the art of talking on this occasion and was only unsure of something he repeated at the end of their exchange. 'Gou Anme' he said while holding up one of the dried leaves to his mouth. It was only years later did she learn that it meant 'bitter taste' in Haitian Creole.

Snake Beat PT IX

Re-form,

I think about how I'll
etch out a more
Nubian version of
alternative
histories and
kingdoms
beyond this
map's traces for
my daughter.
I think about the
odes to earth in
reggae music.

Re-birth,

Re-form.

Trans-gress,
Trans-cribe,
Trans-late,
Trans-ition,
Trans-gress,
Trans-cribe.

Complex Hive communication: A note

Honeybees have a way of talking to each other like no other living thing; they give each other directions to the location of food and nutrients by staging a performance known as 'The Waggle Dance'. The nest may be dark in its depths but there the honeybee physically vibrates to signal news. Her vibes ricochet across the honeycomb and ripple thanks to her wiggle and waggle, telling hungry co-workers, comrades, peers, friends and family the route. Her dance heightens to spins in the shape of the figure of eight in continuous rhythm, wiggling and waggling as she goes, giving direction from her abdomen to the direction of food to the other bees and depending on which way she points her head, the other bees know how far the food might be and whether to fly towards or away from the sun and before the hungry foragers leave on their expedition for sustenance they remember the specific smell of the flowers on the dancing bee, in order to sniff their way to the exact flora the waggling bee is pointing out. Communicating ideas so abstractly is extraordinary among animals who mostly rely on smell or sight.

Chapter Threads

magical realism – a genre of storytelling where the fantastical and extraordinary are told as completely natural fact.

between my thumb and forefinger – an acupressure point used to relieve tension, headaches and other bodily aches.

scotch bonnets – scotch bonnet peppers get their name from their distinct shape, that bears resemblance to a Scottish Tam o' Shanter cap.

Xaymaca – the original name for the island of Jamaica is the Taíno translation for 'land of wood and water'.

11

Betty Davis

Singer, songwriter, troubadour

'. . . the only advice I have is be true to your art form. And by that, I mean do what's in your heart more so than what's in your head.'

Betty Davis in *Dazed* Magazine

Born: 26 July 1944
Died: 9 February 2022
Sign: Leo
Pronouns: She / Her

Betty Gray Mabry was born in North Carolina on 26 July 1944, under the astrological Leo sign, symbolised by a lion and characterised by courage. Just like the bees, Betty waggled, communicating to us all that there's sweet life available to us should we want it, one where women could roar as catharsis, and have agency over their sexuality beyond the male gaze.

Betty was badassery personified. Her performances were those of a lioness, in her Leo fire.

She was unapologetically sexual, in a way that seemed to come from her and not through wanting to be attractive to men.

When Betty grew up in the southern states of North America in the 1940s and 1950s, the spectre of forced labour still hung over the land around her. Freedom for Black, formerly enslaved people was still being invented as she grew up. And yet there had to be ways of reminding her cells and those of people around her of our inherited power to thrive. Could emancipation be embodied in faith, for example? Faith in a god or faith in a music? Was freedom scored in the rebellious sound of the blues? A style of release, by design. Imaginative storytelling at its most moving. A nu language // lore connecting generations of the harmed, an invitation to express truth. A musicality that allowed the dexterity of Black folk to expel painful memories through fingers and into the metal strings of the guitars the players held against their guts, and the singers in unison cast activations for all who listened. A music that could help us to think differently about ourselves beyond what white supremacy would have us believe. Black communities had not long been freed from forced slavery. Fifty years of emancipation might have sounded like a lot on paper. But Black people were still meeting the barriers of segregation on a daily basis. Most public spaces were still for 'Whites Only'. Black neighbourhoods were kept poor, even though they were rich in resistance, even if that act of resistance meant maintaining strong family values and being kin-focused, showing how nurture itself can act as a safe grounding from the hostility and ongoing trauma of racism. If we receive love from our community then the practice of self love grows from the same root.

A lot of survival at that time depended on devotion and faith – guided by church life and the Baptist gospel. Sense, sound and vision. There's a language in the rapturous sonics of hymns in the Gospel Churches (also known as Praise Halls) of mid-twentieth-century America.

This was the world in which Betty Davis was forged.

As a young child Betty was introduced to music by her grandmother, Beulah, on her farm, in Reidsville, which sits north of the state of North Carolina and has 'Live Simply, Think Big' as the local motto. Imagine no screens, just sound; the crackles of guitar-heavy and whip-smart blues played out on the wireless in late 1940's Reidsville, with views of green open space from your window.

You can feel the people who influenced her. She grew up in a part of the world pollinated with the beauty of Black creativity. Betty would listen to the multi-instrumentalist genius of Jimmy Reed, an artist who taught himself to play both harmonica and guitar between bouts of epileptic fits. It's also where she heard the visionary lyrics of **B.B. King**. Betty listened to the sonic invention of the Blues as a child, and for the first time was offered remedy and inspiration from pioneers and dreamers like her; dreamers who weren't shown linear and instructional routes to a life of financial security or physical safety, dreams and sounds taking them beyond the labour forced on countless generations before them. While the Blues played, sensuous ways of understanding were revealed; listeners were informed of a new gaze. Because, yes, the melancholy which birthed blues music can be heard and felt, and there's a bigger journey in the genre: repertoires act as musical guides to take us from ache-to-connection-to-comfort. And it's this that gives the Blues its magnetism. Black music in its full power tends to our wounds and that's why it's loved for eternity. And it's in the artistry that the magic lies. By age 12, Betty had been inspired enough to have written her own first song, 'I'm Going To Bake That Cake Of Love'.

How is it that the timbre and timelessness of voices of the Southern states are so resonant for so many of us? What is it within the potency of accents that, when we hear them, they can make a human heart sing still now? I believe our love of accents to be rooted in an aural reminder that home can be found in our bodies, wherever we may be. Aural connection is intuitive, as is time and space. Aural cartography stretches us to places we've never lived and still have us sense 'home'. Can accents somehow remind us that we are not alone?

The Technology of Fashion

Aged 16, Betty and her family relocated in the Homestead borough of Pittsburgh in Pennsylvania. From there, she travelled to New York City to enrol at FIT (The Fashion Institute of Technology, originally founded in 1944) which focused on art, business, design, mass communication and technology, connected specifically to the fashion industry.

The Blues influence migrated with her. She spent time with the likes of **Sly Stone** among the artsy crowd of the renowned, impeccably hip Greenwich Village bar, 'The Cellar'. She'd spend days and nights conversing with models, poets, design students of different backgrounds and races, and, importantly, dropping tunes.

I'll never underestimate the skill it takes to curate music and provide a vibe in a place that makes the public gravitate to it. It's one of my lifelines of sheer joy, to press play on a jam that gets folk grooving, to guide the vibrations and melody in our bodies as we make memories, cook ideas and fall in love.

To DJ in the right place, at the right time, is to create collective alchemy.

Like the coils and kinks we share in the hair Betty and I both chose to wear natural, I too am obsessed with gravitational glamour and the trappings of fashion. Betty wasn't afraid of the loudness in the clothes she chose to wear. Photos of her in her get-up and swag during her formative times in New York have me delighted. Patchwork, snakeskin, huge pointed lapels, and those over-the-knee, thigh-high, silver boots, to name but a few of her desirable garments.

I'd like to bop, arm-in-arm as sisters, walk on the Lower East Side in 1969 with co-ordinated parasols. I want to immortalise Betty in collage, with her effervescent smile, her Afro, all of her infectious artistry. Because her style lends itself to a study of an ancient technology. Yes, fashion is a technology, but one of tactile spirit-fused and potential invigoration. Her legacy makes me want to think about how great style is the artisan's lore and has been throughout the history of time, connecting the sisters in their immortality.

It takes one afternoon of a Betty Davis listening immersion to become intoxicated by her drawl and, at the same time, be given an opportunity to time travel. She howls for **Chuck Berry**, shouts out her grandad listening to the blues and drinking moonshine in her most notorious track and tag line, 'They Say I'm Different'. Generously offering a sound education. It's a tactic she used in her defining track, 'F.U.N.K', in which she roll-calls Tina Turner, Al Green, Barry White, Isaac Hayes and Jimi Hendrix, whose name she sings over and over after pointing out the velocity of feeling he had in his hands.

> She was indomitable – she couldn't be tamed. Musically, philosophically and physically, she was extreme and attractive.
>
> Carlos Santana[1]

Timely Inventions

> Miss Davis is trying to tell us something real and basic about our irrational needs, and Western civilization puts its highest premiums on conformity and rationality and rarely recognizes the Bessies or the Bettys until they're gone.
>
> *The New York Times*, 1974

In the late 1960s, shifts and waves of change simultaneously occurred all over the world. Colonialism was starting to crumble in many African nations, and some of the most masterful genres of music I know were coming into being. In Ghana, for one, people were expressing their liberty through a social boom and the momentous party sounds of High Life. The scene saw Ghanaian cities erupt with a love in the air so strong that, in the cavernous halls commissioned by the English elite to entertain themselves with 'big band' processions, saw Ghanaian people reclaim in their thousands to dance to High Life instead. Following their independence in 1957, droves of Ghanaians – professionally coiffed and glammed-to-joyful perfection, in shoes so shiny that sparks like moonbeams bounced off them – danced until the sun came up with every tap and every twirl of the diminishing negative effects of the British Empire. This lasted well into the late 1970s.

Can you imagine how creative Black people in the USA had to be feeling in order to create funk music? Many of the scene's originators were living in the cities where the children of those born into forced labour for a number of generations had gone to seek better lives. Slavery had only been outlawed one hundred years before. Synth, electric guitar, bass, fringed leather, all created human symbols of motion, intergalactic paraphernalia, to create a vibe so penetrating to the soul that it made its way from dive basements in Manhattan to garages in Chicago, to the carpeted pubs in the midlands in England where some of my own family were inspired to create bands that sounded like **Earth, Wind and Fire**. Whatever was going on, funk was resonating on a new frequency, with Afros aplenty, rapturous pride, and androgynous mash-ups of garments in purple, constellation prints, inches of lapels and exquisitely ironed flared suits.

It feels so lovely to think of creatives feeling joy when making their art, the visceral and good vibrations pulsating through the act of imagining, writing, painting and others responding whenever they have come across funk. I've felt exaltation in the music of Betty, in the funk genre and its wild inventive mash-ups of sequins and sequences, verve, edge, synth and electric guitars bonding jazz, metal and disco and heart of soul. I would go to the church of funk and praise.

Betty's music enticed its listeners to access the primality of delicious pleasure and agency in their sexuality. How do we feel good? How do we claim ownership of our bodies as womxn, with the gaze of bad men seeping in?

Can we literally 'shake out' interalised misogyny?

Sexual agency

I was describing to my love the infiltration of the patriarchal bias in standards of beauty and value and self-worth. When you feel your image is subject to debate by the mainstream, it's physiologically damaging. To etch a framework of confidence and embodied sense of self is something I've found only later in life, and with thorough assessment of my relationship to sex, love, dating, photos and transformation. These understandings were not encouraged in my education and in the formation of a young woman in the 90s growing up in the Global North, with heritage that takes me from Scotland to the Global South. I was also, as I point out time and time again in this book, formed in the looseness of the 1990s and 2000s.

Recently I wound up watching a film called *The Rules of Attraction*, adapted from a book of the same name from 2002.

I was with a group of cherished friends and there we were, soaking up what Netflix had to offer on a break in the countryside in search of some heart warmth and nostalgia. The film started with a rape scene and went on to glamourise suicide and hardcore drug-taking. The only Black character in the film happened to be a drug dealer's accomplice and have a Jamaican accent. Each young woman in the film was a UK size 0–8, white with straight hair, and obsessed with the validation of being attractive enough to have sex with, the sex being with young men who did not seem to question the nefarious and misogynistic lifestyle they portrayed. It made us sad.

When I was growing up, I remember thinking for hours about how I could straighten my Afro hair to be 'better looking'. There simply were no beautiful women around me with natural Afro hair; no one in the magazines I bought or on TV, except for 'Scary Spice', who was, let's be honest, called 'Scary Spice' and stereotyped as brash and over-the-top amongst her band members. I'm mad about that – why was the era of my youth so steeped in misogyny and racism and why has that feeling insidiously followed me around until uncomfortably unpicked and examined head on?

Betty, her rip-roar, her grunts, grooves and performance style, are still revolutionary all these decades later. She was unapologetic, and she embedded her revenge for all the ways she had been mistreated as a woman and as a Black woman right there in her lyrics. If music can create new and empowering paradigms, catch us unawares and reflect back the truth of how hard we can be on ourselves, and show us how we compare ourselves so often to the capitalist and pornified image we are presented, then Betty's music was a lasting revolt in sound.

It makes sense that during her musical career Betty spent time in London and travelled to the opposite coasts of the US. When listening to her back catalogue, I find it jaw-dropping to note the many genres she straddled and triumphed in creating as a musician. London has always been the best melting pot of influences to draw from. In London, like no other place in the world, you'll experience a vibe completely different in the flat downstairs, and at the next tube stop. In London Betty befriended Marc Bolan and they'd nerd-out on songwriting.

Her career was so permeated with a sense of seeking: seeking ownership in her creative process to make the music, and seeking the autonomy she required in what would be the end product of her art. A powerful role the music industry was / is not designed to offer artists. She wanted control of her work and she – quite literally – had to travel the globe to find it.

Independently Blue

Betty was a virtuoso in music, and the most prominent woman responsible for taking jazz and alchemising it with funk and psychedelic.

If the blues were laments you could dance to, then tracing its evolution to funk music during the 1960s and 1970s is the archive of Black life and scholarly pursuit I seek, and Betty Davis's work is some of the most compelling I have ever had the privilege to fill my own mind and body with. I believe that Betty loved her audience, too.

Betty's keyboardist and vocalist, Fred Mills, described how they never learned in 'key' and that structure or formality wasn't important when they made music together. It was about rehearsing and feeling the vibes. The songs were conjured through trough foot-stomping, vibing and Betty's deep ideas. Taking the strictness away from artistic process excites me. I think when we let rip, that's when the magic happens.

In her song 'Politician Man', Betty compels in her signature seductive snarl, with riddle-like lyrics that mimic a sleazy politician enticing a woman into his car:

'I support the women, though I'm leanin' to the right'.

It was produced by Miles Davis and at the beginning you hear him ask her to sing the song with 'the gum in her mouth.' She would have been 23 years old at the time and he would have been 43. It's clear he would've been aware of her rare and luminous talent. In the documentary about her life, Betty speaks about how she sorted out Miles's style and, specifically, improved his taste in shoes! Some would argue she invigorated his music, too. You can actually chart that it's after he met Betty that his music became way more languid, more psychedelic and experimental. It's truly a shame that the projection of his own demons was what Betty ended up getting from him in return.

Betty began dating Miles in early 1968, and they were married in September that year. In just one year of marriage, she influenced him greatly by introducing him to the latest fashions and the new music trends of the era. In his autobiography, Miles credited Betty with helping plant the seeds of his future musical explorations by introducing him, as a trumpet player, to the psychedelic majesty of Jimi Hendrix's guitar playing and to funk-innovating Sly Stone. The Miles Davis album *Filles de Kilimanjaro* (1968), which features a portrait of Betty on the cover, includes a song named after her – 'Mademoiselle Mabry (Miss Mabry)'. Betty was born with the surname Mabry, acquiring the 'Davis' upon marriage.

Miles had a violent temper and would often get jealous and accuse Betty of having an affair with her friend Hendrix, which hastened the end of their marriage. In his autobiography, Miles said Betty was 'too young and wild'. After accusing her of adultery, he filed for divorce in 1969 – they were married for a little over a year.

'Every second of that marriage I earnt my name', she said, alluding to the suffering she was said to have endured at Miles's hands. The grounds of their divorce was 'temperament on his part'. I can only imagine, based on her lyrics alone, what aggression Betty must have endured.

My heart breaks again at a truth of abuse so often baked into the stories of greatness. And yet I'm inclined to focus on Betty's survival: her irreverence in the face of adversity. Betty sang the blues wrapped in the sounds of pungent and compelling funk.

Having the funk

Mapping the expression of the Sistxrhood

How did both Betty, who moved to New York City in 1960 as a teenager, and Marsha P. Johnson, who left home for the same city three years later aged 18, both African American and both outsiders with frankly genre-defying style, feel out their flair? What did they see on the streets that inspired their courage to party, to play and sashay, in Betty's case in patchwork leather with a giant Afro, and in Marsha's with flowers in her hair and sequins adorning her body?

I discover clues reading about the history of dance and liberation on the African continent. La Sape, a movement in 1920s Congo, was a scene of erudite dandies, born out of vibrant sartorial expression and a will to live beyond obedience: the obedience expected of them and forced upon them when faced with the command to be 'civilised' in the eyes of colonisers. 'Se Saper' (a

French colloquialism meaning to dress 'with class') came out of that experience. This was during the French colonial years in what was then known as the Congo; the French authorities tried to inculcate European-style civilisation by bringing in pre-worn clothes from France and trading them with people to get the population all dressing in the same conformist attire. Some exquisite dandies, instead, reappropriated that attitude and made it their own.

I feel so many of our Sisterhood did the same in their disobedience, in their style of dress and the art they made. When Betty roared on stage like a lion in ecstasy she sonically boomed an invitation for us all to find our own sexuality on our own terms. When Grace Jones is the subject of a photo shoot and builds surrealism mastery by using props like hats and hula hoops she reinforces the super-powered clown in us all and dares us to live as jubilantly.

The Black bohemians of the funk scene evoked elegance and ease, and wore couture-like items as an act of living visual delight and refinement for our eyes – the colours vivid, the attention to detail magnetic, their movement almost shamanic, with all that infectious flair.

When I think of the artistry of Betty I note that what she did was and still is so unique and expansive that it's impossible to grasp in the English language. Betty's songs and her performance of them make you want to move – plain and simple. When we move we are not obedient or contained, we embrace the kinetics and somatic feeling available to us at all living times.

Eventually, Betty disappeared from the scene. I can understand why she stepped back from public view. I can only hope, from the basis of my personal knowledge of the toll of being rejected multiple times, that she found leisure and sanctuary when she entered her period of hermitage.

A Sense Memory: Baby Gem

I'm decluttering.

I rummage and chuck, rummage and chuck, and hold up my possessions like archaeological artefacts. I have to admit I've collected lots of life. I have knick-knacks holding instant memories engraved into my soul of travels. Books upon books upon notepads upon journals, some of which have saved my life a few times, others filled with poetic grasping, some moving, some garbled and full of fury. Love letters. Badges. Clipboards and other stationery that have made me better at my job. Post-its scrawled with numbers / ideas from manic moments, desperately trying to be organised.

Style, clothes, image and energetic identity have brought me and all those that have set eyes on me a lot of entertainment over the years. A life so far spent dreaming in clothes, touching textiles and reinventing through threads, a love for the essence of fashion. In my early twenties, roots took hold in the magazine culture around me, living in a very specific time, at the pin in the map of 'trendy' East London.

I declutter printed-out photographs that I've carefully had printed and stored, in protest at the devices that usually store them.

'All this soul searching one's susceptible to,' I think, lots of it is symbolised in '*my style*'. An exterior, beaming out what might be going on inside. Different and significant chapters have been framed by many . . . outlandish expressions of cloth or shoes so hard to walk in, I simply must have a higher pain threshold than I sometimes give myself credit for.

So many stages in heels.
Metallics,
leather,
zips,

brighter than bright hosiery,
angular shapes
not forgetting deep berry lips . . . all have been experimented with upon my body
never the wallflower

a flower yes, I adore them, but I identify more with the wild roses that bloom big in colours of fire rather than the 'English Rose'.

I did grow up a woman, formed in En-ger-land, after all . . .

The syllables were chanted in the streets. I once so loudly and proudly got a more 'high-street-fashiony' version of an England football strip customised with the lettering to spell out . . . 'KINKY G' upon my back, as I thought it was the funniest and most outrageous nickname to give myself when coming up with nicknames for one another on a girls' trip to Tenerife aged 18.

Oh the fucking nineties.
cheaply made clothing

disasters
all this experimental adolescence and thrilling unfolding of my own modern history
has made me in the past happy.
I buy something new once a year these days.

'You cannot wear that, Gem,' said my co-presenter once.
'Why?' I asked.

'Because you'll make me look really boring.'

I'm so glad to have learned that clothes can be POWER.

How courageous it must have been to write, record and perform as an alternatively-dressed Black woman with mixed heritage in the 1960s and 1970s, singing and dancing to these sexually-sonic riffs. Betty screamed poetic-resilience and chorus-erotica through her lyrics, proclaiming herself a 'nasty gal' and performing in thigh-high silver boots while challenging the abusive nature of politicians and reclaiming the power of seduction in song-form.

WE
SEE
YOU
BETTY

Womxn who make expressive art that makes people feel things are dangerous, are 'othered' time and time again, or worse quashed. But the smarts of Betty are preserved in the most powerful brew of all – the portal of song and the capturing of her performances.

Davis's last recording, in 1979, saw her retrace geography and move back to Pittsburgh, Pennsylvania, where some of her **lightning strikes** had started. She retreated to a quiet life and it is hard, even today, to find the archive and repertoire of her work that she deserves as a musical pioneer who has inspired so many of today's greatest artists. She put the funk into Miles Davis, a musician who's received accolade after accolade. But what is it about Betty that stops our society, obsessed with history and nostalgia, from referring to the source and true raw inspiration? I would argue that when we face the reality that her life was marred by the patriarchy it makes us uncomfortable to our core. Do we only now have the capacity to say that perhaps we've been getting it wrong, by disproportionately praising the achievements of men? I think so. I wonder if practicing reverence is a way of setting myself free?

Just before Christmas 2023

Asheville

Dear Betty

I'm writing this in a library in Asheville, North Carolina.

I'm here because since meeting a great love with dual citizenship in both the States and in the UK, I've visited North America differently. I've been opened up to new places. I'd only ever heard of the Carolinas in films before now. But here I am, in the birthplace of Thelonious Monk, George Clinton, Nina Simone and . . . you. Where the sounds and revelry of Scots / crackers and Irish bards blend in with the rapture of the blues, and the strings of instruments vibrate with a calling for transformation. Did you hear that same call, Betty? Did you hear wanderlust in vibrations of Jimmy Reed when you heard him played on your grandparents' farm?

I'm in the local library, where vagabonds come to be and pass the time of day, it seems. Homelessness in America, they say, has gotten real bad. Politics are in disarray and healthcare not being free is felt in a place like this. What were the vagabonds like in your day? Many of them, I'm sure, you would have come across in New York once you moved from Pennsylvania. One of my favourite cities in the world. I wonder what you thought of it? Whether you missed the native magnolia trees or the subterranean weather of midsummers as a child? Was the Cherokee heritage that made some of your blood part of the reason you went on in later life to describe yourself as an amoeba? An ever-changing phenomenon of music, able to channel, orchestrate and harmonise a genre-defying cardinal desire to express our sexual selves, to cathart with roar and fire? Burn the exploitation of our womanly ancestors, who birthed us through genocidal attempts to eradicate our kind? Do those of us with mixed roots grow with morphing abilities in our guts? By surviving in so many surroundings and creating fusion so naturally, do we in fact have a superpower, despite navigating all the othering we have faced?

I know you spent time in London in the early and late 1970s. I've heard references that it was pretty smelly back then? Apparently Bob Marley couldn't stand the stench of the punk scene when he first spent time in the capital. But he came round by sheer force of energy and anti-establishment drive . . . and wrote 'Punk Reggae Party' (one of my faves) in 1977. Did you ever listen to reggae? Secretly I feel reggae is as healing as any gong bath when listened to where it hits the body.

Did your lovers buy you flowers? I really hope they did.

All my love

Snake Beat PT X

I bow my head and
bounce in honour of
the word play and
poetry of patois.
Re-birth,

Re-form,

I see new routes.

A Sense Memory: Rememberings and confusion

Remember when the printing of photos was precious?

Remember when the kooky, the different and the rambunctious were the mainstream's north star?

Remember when your emails may have had a heartfelt letter in there and not just marketing from a company using overfamiliar language?

Remember when you had to call your friends to find out how they were?

Remember when a hotel was a place to stay and offer comfort that may have been recommended to you by word-of-mouth, rather than a 'place to be seen' made virtual via a hashtag or review?

Remember when striking up a conversation with someone at a bus stop / on a train was likely to be a positive experience?

Remember before 'being a hipster' was a thing?

Remember when banking was a physical act?

Remember cash?

Remember when working freelance represented something 'free' and independent?

Remember when the word anxiety wasn't in our vocabulary / was maybe considered by the beholder as excitement?

A Sense Memory: DEEP ERASURE

People confide in me, they always have. In this case a brave peer emails me about the emotional repercussions of some mistreatment they've experienced during a summer working on a particular project that they've been building for a long time. They've had a hard time bringing it into fruition for various reasons, including lack of funding. They start out by describing the experience as generally 'upsetting', and go on to explain some details . . . Then there are two words that stop me in my tracks, 'deep erasure', 'there has been some deep erasure happening'. They write and I'm stopped in my tracks,

in this moment,

into connection {no distraction // no denial // dissonance vanishes},

into their reflection, into resonant solidarity. I've not heard mistreatment in a working situation described in such terms before, but I have heard and felt the same flavour of hurt from many.

Because erasure is at its deepest when it occurs after so much work has already been done. When our minds and bodies are asked to over-whir, in systems that make us justify our existence, our relevance, our dreams and duty, again and again, in order to make a living in a life where many of us are forced to be desperate to live well (the clue being the word living). Deep erasure undermines the genesis of the idea / the seed of hope; which is maddening for the thinkers who thrive in solution and innovation based practice, only for a jury called dissonance to throw imagination to the wastelands through the lack of support, resource or even recognition of the bodies and souls that have put in so much time and effort to produce cultural ambition.

I have seen this happening to artists / producers / writers / visionaries so much in my life. The truly luminous ones that might even have a shot at changing something in the world can be hindered all too easily, sometimes by buried disapproval of stepping into their greatness (a common effect of abusive / neglectful relationships, including romantic, familial and in work). Sometimes they are burned out so badly by being ignored and unheard that the wonder from which they conjured their work gets worn down or at worst eliminated altogether. Everyone needs care for their ideas, even the 'weirder' folk whose minds might be on the fringes and beyond typical thinking patterns, or the folk who grew up poor and didn't get encouragement to go beyond the struggle for survival but had their imagination gobbled up by capitalism all the same. The nurturing part of the process of growing a better world requires a constant flame-tending of positive force from all corners of society – the opposite of cancelling or erasing culture. And we need to all become committed to strengthening diverse pioneers. There are those full of fire in their love for humanity and their belief in healing, in a rawness that is not driven by dominance, violence, ghettoising or greed but by activism. There are those whose passion for writing, making and storytelling could unleash the unity and craft within us all, for the better. There are those who were forced to seek belonging in the movement of water and notice that the life lines in the palms of their hands look the same as those on leaves and who are drawn to mythic and esoteric language despite being commonly demonised as strange. They know how much the land is needing our attention as much as its people are. They are the ones who really know the mutual love of plants and of self-soothing with folklore (perhaps even guided there because their caregivers couldn't offer them what the natural world can, or they never had access to wisdom passed down to them . . . We must listen). There are those who have both quiet discipline and knowingness, without needing fame or popularity, some of whom have had to pull themselves back from the edges they have been cast out to, in towers of hierarchy that deem people that don't look like them less important and worthy, while those who work at the fringes, the geniuses and artisans making life from what they can and emanating SO MUCH excellence that everyone else could learn from, those people are almost never paid what they should be. How can we allow for the silencing of this progressive greatness that goes on and the deep erasure that follows? How are we not demanding more positivity for the masses and valuing the wild and the brave ones creating it? Where did the work leading up to now go? All the archives, databases, books, poems, photographs and songs written . . . ? When did our sacred appreciation become collective amnesia? Where we can find ourselves ruminating on the negative and grotesque?

For those who continue to work, to make and to educate, use their hands, to write, gather folk, organise and value culture . . . despite how gruelling it can feel in these times we're in; for those of us who keep on keeping on // when the expectation of the industry is that everything should be new all of the time – I see you! Because it seems that thinking something is happening for the first time makes us all special – but instead it actually keeps us 'pedestalling' the chosen few and making 'the few' rich with opportunity. We must remember that the algorithms, data and the AI responses and gatekeeping often keep us all separated and wanting more and needing it all so quickly. When it is all there for us, written in history, asking for us to learn patience and appreciate and look around us at who's really got the best intentions for a future where we are all free. We must not erase our truest tools of salvation, because they are within us; they stem from our hearts, a source of practice and creativity.

I have cycled from London to Paris. I have had books published and have interviewed some of the most profound living thinkers – from contemporary artist Marina Abramović to astronaut Colonel Chris Hadfield – but I'm still spending so much time fighting to be heard. I've learned a lot about the human condition in my untypical route here and still only really know three root causes to my insatiability: a belief in representation, a need for love and, if I'm honest, a fear of being forgotten.

In an interview with inimitable African American writer Toni Morrison recorded in 2003, **Charlie Rose** asked her what she would distil into a lecture if it was her last one to give on earth. She said this:

> I would like to say how hard it is and how necessary it is for us to become and to remain humans, that means a lot, it means not giving in to the comic book version of who we are, not giving in to all this medieval rhetoric . . . but doing what we know deep down what's right and what's true and what's needed . . . we got to get there, we just have to.

Toni said this in a TV interview long before our so-called AI 'boom'. There was a sense back then of existential scrabbling for our purpose and human-ness and now we have to contend with resorting to computers to help us try and remember what is to be human. But what if we were to look at this quote from the late Toni Morrison as a simple invitation to fall back in love with ourselves, our whole selves – with our imperfections and the quirks that defy logic but make us human. What if we were to choose love in the light of day and in the dark. In this context, I would take it a step further and suggest that in order to do such a thing, we could try honouring the survival of those who continued to make great lives despite being ostracised. I'd add the 'what if' . . . we were to look around ourselves and allow the truth to be shown that so much senseless hatred is projected because of capitalism and patriarchal constructs that empower some of the human race to flourish and thrive and not others? Would the reframing of history and understanding help us to move beyond the torment of some of this dehumanisation and hatred into awe? Into resilience and into love? For many of us it would be moving beyond the medieval rhetoric that Toni

Morrison warns us of and into a radical, riotous human redemption. We would find ways to protect women in all our breadth. It would be exactly the 'the right and true' that she prompts us all to find in our current lifetimes.

In Saidiya Hartman's *Wayward Lives, Beautiful Experiments: Intimate Histories of Riotous Black Girls, Troublesome Women and Queer Radicals*, she notes her method in the book to be one:

> crafted as a counter narrative liberated from the judgement and classification that subjected young black women to surveillance, arrest, punishment and confinement, and offer an account that attends to beautiful experiments – to make living art – undertaken by those often described as promiscuous, reckless, wild and wayward. The endeavour is to recover the insurgent ground of these lives; to exhume open rebellion from the case file, to untether waywardness, refusal, mutual aid, and free love from their identification as deviance . . .

This leads me to point out that the protection and the disruptive potential of our Sisterhood cannot be erased, and nor can its central concept – because SISTXRHOOD is shapeshifting and everywhere. The immortality of the Sisterhood is in the journeys we choose that retrace the footsteps of women thousands of years ago and the freedom with which we to choose to express ourselves and in how we present ourselves to the world, and how our work is so often drawn from the inspiration we take from our friends, our family, our kinfolk, our mentors, mothers and their mothers, our ancestors – The 'hood. We are never alone when we embrace this and it strengthens our ability to rise above any attempt of deep erasure.

I hereby mark my loyalty to anti-erasure in the roots of this sisterhood as we approach the final chapter of this literary experiment. As with this process of creation, I bear no capitalist or academic expectation except to embrace an unbridled discovery that we may share in decolonising history and our memories and move through this to collectively craft a critical response to received history. The type that vibrates our bellies.

Chapter Threads

B.B. King – a blues guitarist, singer and songwriter born in Mississippi, USA in 1925.

Sly Stone – a singer and songwriter at the vanguard of funk, as the lead singer of Sly and the Family Stone, born in Texas, USA in 1943.

Chuck Berry – a pioneer of rock 'n' roll, a guitarist, singer and songwriter born in St. Louis, USA in 1926.

Earth, Wind and Fire – a funk band formed in the United States in 1969, spanning soul, funk, disco and pop.

lightning bolts – a cosmic and elemental ideas moment.

Charlie Rose – American journalist and talk show host from the early 1990s to 2017, when his show was cancelled amid sexual harassment allegations.

Snake Beat PT XI

Diaspora
leading to
re-volution
Mango, sunset, MOON,
The time I stared at the
Caribbean sea on the edge of
my island to rageful waves
after a night storm
'Tis her time of the month' said
the man raking the debris
washed up
I howled, with laughter

Reeeeeeeeclaimation, re-wilding lands

Words dance brightly the R's still roll

RESTORE

rrrrrrrevitalise

Healing civilizations.

'Many of us of third generation of
atrocity, I've found . . . End up
with surging senses of justice'
Says a friend over a lightning-bolt
lunch.

RRRrrrrrrrEPARATIONS.

12

Pharaoh Hatshepsut

Gender-defying leader who excelled in architectural advancement, travel and trade and overcoming trauma

'Her fragrance was like divine breath, skin is made of gold, it shines like stars'

Hatshepsut, describing herself

Born: 1505–1495 BCE
Died: 1458 BCE
Sign: Unknown
Pronouns: She / Her / They / Them

Hatshepsut was a genderless Pharaoh who ruled for approximately 15 years between 1479 BCE and 1458 BCE. With the scant evidence available, we are faced with the delicious puzzle of working out what we think we know of the decisions she made during her rule and how many of her choices were unprecedented and remarkable. She did all her pioneering thousands of years ago, before any of our other sisters – proving that we have always been defying what was expected of us. This is woven into *The Immortal Sisterhood* like a golden thread, again and again.

How was Hatshepsut genderless? Well, you'll notice they are referred to in this chapter with both She / Her and They / Them pronouns – this is because she documented her time on earth doing exactly that, experimenting and fluidly using both feminine and masculine definitions, all to morph into an otherworldly part-god by the time they died. Pretty bold and binary-rejecting behaviour, if you ask me. The exact details aren't available to us in the study of her life but the clues she left to mark out her character are all boldly planted in history. It is also important to remember that her reign was around 1,500 years before that of Cleopatra – arguably the best known Egyptian ruler and somewhat glamourised in contemporary culture because she was a rare woman leader. I'll go on to refer to 'Egypt' as Kemet as we further think about Hatshepsut's iconicism.

Kemet was the word the indigenous of the land themselves used (whereas the name Egypt only really came into use when it started being colonised). Kemet means Black Land, referring to the rich, dark soil that spreads from the River Nile when it floods every year, creating fertile ground for food that at the time couldn't be grown anywhere else in the world.

Hatshepsut's cross dressing was not simply something she wore (she is said to have worn beards made with goats' hair and braided with gold) but something inhabited through stance / masculine mannerisms and posture. Depictions of her show her in strong poses not associated with women but with kings. There have been many statues found of them kneeling, and holding emblems associated with male kings, including the crook, flail and ankh. The shepherd's crook symbolises kingship;

the flail symbolises fertility of the land; and the ankh represents eternal life.

SYMBOLS + CLUES

I have been interested in the Ankh symbol ever since I saw it worn in massive ring form on neo-soul singer Erykah Badu in the early noughties, when I first became such a huge fan of her music and alternative, earthly style. Ancient Kemet has been embedded in the storytelling of many powerful and boundary pushing artists of our time in a number of ways. Hatshepsut is celebrated in hip-hop culture in a duet called 'Hatshepsut' by a rapper called **Rhapsody** and **Queen Latifah**. Our pharaoh holds space for lyrics of U-N-I-T-Y, sisterhood, invites all of us to consider our queendom, and reminds us how when we step up to our potential majesty we hold a torch for our community as equal royalty, considering everyone Kings and Queens . . . we inevitably rise through the act of mutual respect.

Hatshepsut's power threads through soul music, hip-hop ingenuity and even the genre-defying rock / pop of Tina Turner. In 1977 Tina Turner had an encounter with a psychic who told her she was the Pharaoh Hatshepsut in a former life! Tina's track – 'I Might Have Been Queen' refers to this on her multi-selling hit album – *Private Dancer*.

Born into a royal lineage abundant with brothers, Hatshepsut grew up in the shadows. Yet this absence became their power: they rewrote their destiny, sculpting an identity that defied convention. When Thutmose II passed, leaving a child too young to rule, Hatshepsut ascended – not merely as a regent but as Pharaoh.

With audacious brilliance, they declared their divine ascent, throughout their reign agilely weaving a legend as vivid as the painted walls of their mortuary temple. Which was constructed whilst they were still alive. Tales and sermon of how 'The god Amon,' it was said 'conceived Hatshepsut', and had created them to be 'better than all gods.' Strained to spread amongst her society with momentum. Amon was a prolific deity of the time who was associated with creation. This was not merely a claim of legitimacy but an act of reclaiming cosmic order as the people of those lands at that time understood it.

Hatshepsut spent their reign bringing all kinds of change to Kemet life. They introduced new rituals, particularly around burying and celebrating the dead, and oversaw the introduction of architectural magnificence as well as opening up trade with places the kingdom had never had contact with. Imported myrrh used in ritual practice was one of the results of this new trade. I feel spooked by this reminder of the ageless drive of global trade. Everything has always been moving around, everywhere . . . Forever.

Phallic Obelisks

Hatshepsut famously commissioned two trademark obelisks to be built from pink granite at The Great Temple in Luxor. Each was inscribed with demands that she not be forgotten, and blended both feminine and masculine pronouns to describe her deep devotion to the ancient god Amon. Only one of the obelisks stands today, but it is visited by intrigued visitors and historians still fascinated by her three thousand years on.

Hatshepsut's legacy was largely forgotten for centuries after their death, until remains and artefacts from her tomb were found in the nineteenth and twentieth centuries. In 1828, **Jean-François Champollion** (also known for decoding the Rosetta Stone) visited Hatshepsut's temple and was puzzled to find inscriptions referring to a king marked with feminine grammatical symbols. However, it wasn't until Howard Carter excavated her tomb in 1903 that the full picture of who Hatshepsut had been began to emerge.

But how and why was there an attempt to erase the legacy of this genderless pharaoh? It was kicked off by her successor – Thutmose III. The deep erasure began under his order, by removing Hatshepsut's name from historical documents and destroying any monuments commissioned by her or mentioning anything to do with Hatshepsut. Some say it was because her successor wanted to quash her power, innovation and gender bending, and because Hatshepsut had succeeded in creating prosperity and imprinting a unique style on the culture of ancient Kemet. She had left an undeniable mark.

Others have concluded that natural environmental corrosion of the sites simply 'defaced' her projects, making it hard to make out their origins, and that the building of new constructions over the years meant that some of the elaborate architecture of Hatshepsut's rule became re-purposable material for very different spaces, such as a Coptic Monastery built on the site many years later.

I'm forced to consider my connection to this immortal Sistxr. What is my desire to learn about Hatshepsut and to attempt to archive her legacy from so long ago? It is something to do with the unwavering urge to construct something with lasting impact. I dream of leading a team to make something that's for the greater good, beyond individualism. I ache, for example, to build a sauna big enough to share with my local community. To build in the belief that there's enough space for everyone. You only have to spend some time 'roaming' around the vast, sprawling Highlands of Scotland to wonder why there aren't more people up here, and how five hundred or so miles south folk there's so much disparity amongst folk tightly packed into places with a notion that there is 'no space here for refugees', even for the everyday people fleeing the ravages of wars and seeking refuge for their families. I crave the autonomy to plan human-centred, safe, third, loved space. There would be so many plants and flowers.

I'm also drawn to the sensory / sensuous aspects of Hatshepsut's life. They are said to have oiled their body and to have smelt heavenly (she even said so herself). At that time, frankincense was used as a healing ointment and jasmine was used for boosting mood. How much more sumptuous might life be if we focused on scent and how its properties can transform our moods? Imagine if we had the time to anoint ourselves in chosen oils depending on what we needed in any given moment?

Monuments and power

Though I've yet to see Hatshepsut's obelisk, I've started noticing the shape everywhere. There is a behemoth in the centre of Edinburgh, on Calton Hill, standing 90 ft tall, erected in 1844 and named Martyrs' Monument to honour the five men transported to Botany Bay, Australia. It was a time when 'Egyptian' symbology was deemed the pinnacle of sophistication by the elite authorities and by designers alike. But it is not just the capital city's phallic distraction that some of the truly eccentric link to Egpyt. Approximately two hours north stands Schiehallion the Fairy Hill of Caledonia, or the holy mountain.

I care for yoga, a type that includes repetitive words and chants that soothe my busy brain. I am, however, aware of the finest of lines I dance when approaching my practice. I know that yoga without thought for its origins and what class you choose can seem well-meaning but become violent when commodified and whitewashed // I'm confronted often, with my own potential for complicit erasure and greed in search of redemption and survival in our globalised entanglements. In contrast, in the politics of self-care that Sister Audre so generously taught me to really prioritise, I've not found an activity that can make me as giddy as a 90-minute class with no interruption, filled with absurd moves that emulate animals and have us breathing fire. I persevere with a wish to re-pattern a yearning for humility over status. I'm not a better person for doing yoga, but I am a calmer and more hopeful one. I believe that yoga, stretching, and having an understanding of breath and of our voice can give us some of the peace we seek in the quagmire, and I think it may even be able to shake out some of the trauma trapped in my spine and other joints, the connections of my physical and soul self.

I learn about yoga practised in the times of ancient Egypt. Poses were inscribed on the walls of the pyramids in sequences clearly represented in hieroglyphics. It's called Kemetic Yoga.

As I researched ancient Egypt and its archaeological excavation, I found myself swamped by the wild-eyed and adamantly voiced white men who dominated the field, with their brows dusty from digging up graves. It got me wanting to move my mind in opposite directions. I had almost hallucinogenic visions of ancient Kemet and how it must have been. I felt filled with the image of how these lands steeped in wonder – in the northeasterly part of motherland Africa. Where the Red Sea entices from the land's edge, the same sea they say got its name from the seasonal blooms of a red-brown algae and is water home for some coral reef of up to 7,000 years old that can be found nowhere else in the world. These lands were, for thousands of years, populated with Black and brown people able to be so societally advanced that they constructed perfect pyramids. So advanced that symbols were painted on the walls with carbon, iron oxides, azurite and malachite, natural dyes, leaving us only complicated vibrations and ideas of the life that they lived there, with such spiritual splendour that it had me tripping. Different dimensions were found by boiling blue lotus flowers[1] to sip from clay chalices. Gender, colour, objects, smell . . . all hazed, waved and halcyon, and glistening in golds.

A Reign of Prosperity and Grace

Hatshepsut's reign was a time of flourishing. Unlike their predecessors, who sought dominion through conquest, they restored Egypt's fractured monuments, breathed life into **Thebes**, and expanded infrastructure. Their artistic innovations brought a grace to temples, that actualised their vision of a unique architectural harmony

Trade routes reopened under their careful watch. Hatshepsut's expeditions to the land of 'Punt' (probably somewhere in modern-day Eritrea, Ethiopia or Somalia) became legendary. From this distant, mysterious land, their fleet brought treasures: myrrh, frankincense, ivory, ebony, and aromatic woods. These were not mere riches; they were symbols of connection. On the grounds of Deir el-Bahari, 31 myrrh trees from Punt were planted – the first recorded transplant of trees across nations.

Hatshepsut's mortuary temple, Djeser-Djeseru, stands at the base of sunlit limestone cliffs – where terraces, pools, and gardens mirror the heavens' paradise. Refuge comes from within the spaces and tells of their divine birth, their triumphs, and their vision of eternity.

Sense Memories: Seeing faces, loving places

We are currently living through a time of land-grabbing and greed – waiting for some old guys to let go of their grip on power.

We live and wait for the purge to happen, a shedding of the generational hunger for more from those we are told are 'at the top', who control our algorithms, our laws, our rules, our access to better lives. It makes the tension I notice coursing through my veins stir when I scroll through Instagram and the many disordered realities of late-stage capitalism and the many ways in which we are hypnotised to want to own everything and at the same time be terrified of a Global Majority's complicated discourse towards obtaining a birthright such as a safe and good home.

Property, for example, was once thought of as a place of home for everyone or for public purpose, but now more often than not represents economic and social disparity. There is a notion, due to lack of pensions for our generation that if 'we are to care about our futures, we should invest in property' – an idea so normalised but at the same time with property being so difficult to purchase – that I'm left feeling spat out by a system that is solely accessible via inherited wealth, or the data of a credit score or a full-time wage that doesn't allow much hope for those on the outside, those who didn't get money from their parents to buy a house, or those who are immigrants or refugees, and the generations of those who settled in the places that colonised their homelands. Just how are we all supposed to live fairly and equally, when we can't afford a home, and so many public places – built to be places of welcome, leisure, worship, service or respite – these days sit heavily among us in forgotten towns, dilapidated, taken over by pigeons, or even the well-meaning entrepreneurs who try to hipster-ify and gentrify ole skool sensibilities of community.

In the 1970s and 1980s the UK's capital city, London, became a stomping ground for some of those fleeing the nests from which they felt displaced. The multicultural // queer communities, the makers and the creatives that are the foundations of one of the most enriching and meshed cosmopolitan examples of place in the world found the loopholes in the rules and created a phenomenon of squatting in disused buildings. The mantra, of mending, upcycling and creating comfort for people that couldn't afford convention saw a boom in the creative economy in London. The punk scene and all its rippling sentiment bounced through rave culture and fashion that sold all over the world and design took on a DIY aesthetic that still inspires us today.

In the continuous weave of the concept of immortalising Sisterhood, I start to see links and connections of beauty in history. Rather than choosing to look at monuments or buildings as structures of heaviness and grief, in my spare time like visiting former prisons or places of battle, I experiment with flipping historic fascination to guide me to where beauty has and thought has happened instead. My love for wild and epic places, holistic municipal triumphs and tender restoration grows deeper over the lens of brutality that we're often faced with.

A Sense Memory: Gone swimming – Multi-generational municipality

I beam with joy at the reopening of a former Victorian bath in my neighbourhood called Warrender Park Swim Centre. It was founded in 1886 as private swimming baths for buoyant boffins of the time, it being close by to the esteemed university. It's documented well with black-and-white photographs of competing swimming folk in full bathing suits jumping through rings, making glorious archives for us all, all these years later. When I first moved to a tenement flat a few minutes' walk away, I'd noticed the ornate and regal building, but like many buildings here in Edinburgh it had had too many geometric poles of steel scaffolding erected round it to wrap your head around what it might be like inside. It had been closed for a few years, 'under refurbishment' by the council, but I didn't know what I was missing, so I tried not to think about it. But on the day it reopened I was filled with a shared sense of local pride and delight. Years had passed, a pandemic had been and gone, and families of different nationalities flocked to the open doors of the all-new Edinburgh Leisure spot. A restored Victorian bath with translucent, turquoise ripples to etch onto the minds of those attending their first swimming lesson, brand new gym equipment that no one had sweated on yet, and best of all a small, pool-facing sauna, where everyone sits with their neighbours and shoots the breeze. It was a day of testament to a loving community and inspired me to think of the mastery of caring **municipality** that benefits the people within it. Two old ladies talked about the secrets of being happy in their nineties, shoulder to shoulder with a grey, whistling socialist who had revealingly political tattoos; children giggled at one another in the water and bounded out of changing rooms in brightly-coloured costumes. When their eyes meet, I wonder what their relationships are . . . whether they know one another as neighbours, from nursery, school or just because they were kids and being kids is a time spent in rejoicing and laughter and that knowing it is even funnier when you're kid-to-kid, as their parents caught up and marvelled at how nice it was to see one another, and how they couldn't believe how much their little ones had grown, since it was last open a few years ago. It was all so life-giving and made me yearn for more architectural common ground and more great public spaces. I like to think that this is what Hatshepsut envisioned as they sparked an architectural boom in Kemet and brought sensuality and civic pride to every space.

Their reign reminds us of the infinite ways to exist, to rule, and to love. As their obelisk stands tall at Karnak, its shadow stretching across time, it speaks not of conquest but of connection, not of domination but of harmony. Hatshepsut's legacy endures – a beacon for those who dare to rewrite their own stories.

I imagine: a carnelian kiln-masoned cup sits beside them, filled with freshly pressed wine, as they look into a tinted mirror of rose gold. Smoke from burning frankincense curls and Hatshepsut touches the hair on their face and breaks into a smile as they look into their own eyes. How had they got here? How could being born have differentiated their experience from those working nearby? And how much was the determination to rule taking its toll on their heart and mind? They knew they would never know all these answers, but despite all that was complex in the navigation, the lotus heart inside opened everyday regardless.

March 2025

A full Blood Red Moon in 2025

Dear Hatshepsut

Did you know your rule would inspire research for so many years? This is a letter to you from 3,500 years into the future and I'm happy to tell you that some of the greats that I've been led to in the chain of Sisterhood have drawn inspiration from your reign.

I watched a YouTube clip that said that in the times of ancient Egypt . . . which feels kinda ludicrous writing to you as you won't even know what I'm referring to with those words right? Kemet, I mean Kemet, where you are right now. It also feels kinda silly to brand a period 'times of' when 'the times' I'm referring to were actually a part of global history that's still massively unknown to us and that lasted thousands of years. Anyway, the sensationalism I was drawn to in this YouTube clip was one about trance-like ceremonies that involved water lilies being soaked in wine, everyone getting quite psychedelically high, dancing and maybe making love for a few days. Does this ring any bells?

I've further researched and it seems that sensationalism was the right word to use, an effective one too . . . As many folk now are selling beautifully packaged 'Blue Lotuses' online with claims of wellbeing benefits and psychoactive goodness. I must admit, in a world where sexuality has become one of extremes, an ancient, erotic flower-filled, consensual, sexy hangout does seem more intriguing than what's all too often labelled to me as 'desirable'. But, yeah, an academic in the States called Liam McEvoy found that the actual water lily that would have been found in your time on the beds of the Nile are super duper rare and that lots of the vendors are selling a flower that looks a bit similar but doesn't contain the same compounds at all. He's also found in his work that there was such a thing as a 'Hathoric Festival of Drunkenness' referred to on scrolls where you got very merry and had visions of Hathor (the goddess of love, beauty and fertility).[2] I would love to know more. I've thought a lot about whether there are any benefits to drunkenness in my adulthood but this has left me wondering if we've just lost our way and whether some structure and purpose may make it all the more fun? I'm always looking for what I can learn from ancient lore, you see . . . Are you as intrigued as we are about your life by what the future's like? We don't praise particular gods here but do seem to disproportionately lambast ourselves and one another for any ideas around heritage and faith. We have some festivals, that have been twisted somehow into buying stuff to prove love, and though we're fully aware of that fact we can't seem to help ourselves.

I, on accession, try to live by at least the moon and stars. They seem like a safe enough bet in the gloop. They even seem a more lighthearted (and also ancient) way to look for any kind of meaning as at least the roots of astrology are so universally shared.

Just the other day my horoscope said: 'Surrender! On this blood-red moon, clear your path.' And so I got together with some friends and we sat in my front garden round a fire pit as though we were cast members in *The Craft* (a 1990s classic film about witches, practising a fictionalised form of Wicca).

We 'cleansed' by verbally saying what we no longer needed // wrote it down on bits of paper and burned them in the flames of the fire, then we lit a red candle, which I left surrounded by stones in the gravel. Lo 'n' behold! The candle burned there for four nights, the flame swaying in the wind, doing its absolute finest to offer me astonishment every time I checked it, to find it was still aflame. I really do enjoy the moon and its phases. Moments like this everlasting candle bring me closest to a type of wonder I know shaped my heart as a child.

Look forward to hearing from you.

Chapter Threads

Jean-François Champollion – a French founding figure in the field of Egyptology, who is said to be one of the first to decipher Hieroglyphics.

Rhapsody – US-born rapper born in 1983 and the only woman to feature on Kendrick Lamar's album *To Pimp A Butterfly*.

Queen Latifah – multi-award-winning rapper, actress, film producer and talk show host born in 1970.

Thebes – Ancient city and capital of Egypt / Kemet.

municipality – a term referring to a place and its governing bodies.

AFTERWORD

Scars only form on skin that is alive.

Writing about the Sisterhood has given me the opportunity to critically explore the meaning of womanhood and the narrative of our origins; to deeply think about and cry tears for the unfairly treated, the erased and the lost, and along the way, to sculpt my very own definition of justice through learning. I have given space to the sense-felt and not-always-able-to-be-easily-explained nuance of stories when so much is served up fast and through a patriarchal and colonial lens. I hope to have made some kind of experimental poetic from history.

Reject: Colonialism.

The **C** is for control / Twice a day, I am asked to 'quantify' myself and / or my work. When it's the same thing really and I don't wish to be over-explained or commodified.

O is for **o**ld and for **o**rder seeping insidiously into everyday monotony, casting shadows into dreams/ A group of older people dining next to me scowl /

Being told to 'BE QUIET' / a forever position in the 40 years of contortion
'Pipe down',
'Stay in the (right) lane'.

Shhhhhhhhhhhhhhhhhhhhhhhhhhhhhhhhhhhhhhhhhhhhh-hhhhhame /

punitive paradigms,

L for Longing / Remembering the freedom felt in a fugitive youth / running for my life / when it was all worth playing for / zest catapulting soul from ancient fight and into flight / we borrowed Prende's[1] rainbow for a belt regularly in those times, rode the skies for love not greed. There was no quantification, just momentum, resilience and laughter.

O for Ongoing, a life full of revelation

N for No. All the no's / so many no's / no answer / no more . . . Computer says NO / and there's no time to be embarrassed

I for Indigenous knowledge

A for positive Affirmation, no matter how serious or cheesy it seems

L for Love, the only answer

I for Individual gain

Sunshine has answers and so does silliness

Memories, make them good.

Lots has happened and continues to since I set out creating this book. I've lost beloveds to sickness, I've had relationships drawn to a close in mutuality and respect. Through it all I've noted that studying collective liberation can aid our individual journey towards belonging, and that feeling – sensory memory, wisdom, and imagination – does not ever die.

I hope you'll marvel too at some of the coincidences I noticed. Perhaps you'll notice the open seeking for equality and parity? Perhaps you'll hear the beat and catch the rhythm created for you to read, with our heartbeats in mind. In a time where our attention spans are scattered into fragments of worlds online and off, I ask for you to breathe, be in the quiet of reading and immerse yourself in the beauty of The 'Hood. Feel free to lean on the multiplicity of our soft intentions, keep your mind open and refreshed for hope, kismet and serendipity. I ask if we, as an immortal collective, could make it impossible to erase the tools that have been set out for us. I ask we consider our need for saving the world as also living to our most full and all the while in trusted company.

> The liberation of the earth, the liberation of women, the liberation of all humanity is the next step of freedom we need to work for, and it's the next step of peace that we need to create.
>
> Vandana Shiva, physicist and environmental activist

November 2024

I'm in the middle of a psychic reading down the phone (don't judge me! I'm endlessly looking for answers) and, according to the voice on the end on the line, the scar on my belly is still what she describes as esoterically 'active'. I don't really know what she means in the context of other, psychic realms but I do, physically, in the here and now. Scars remain on my changing skins these days, but embedded cynicism and fear don't. I feel if we're not walking miracles then what are we? It remains a mystery how the psychic knows about the tenderness I feel in the area where I've endured an incision in my abdomen, to remove four fibroids of varying fruit-size, the biggest being as large as a beef tomato. At that moment, I just exhale deeply and nod. My body is a map of my wounds and wonder, and those of my ancestors too.

From the many notations of the wise and divine, I am well versed in the metaphors and secrets that women carry, and the power and stories in their womb. With so much, as it turns out, being under-researched in women's medicine, I have been forced to seek guidance and perspective from more ancient and unruly sources at times. If I had listened solely to the doctors I was being exposed to by the system, I would still have four fibroids, one as large as a beef tomato, lodged deep in and protruding through my stomach, making up a Galapagos of discomfort in the memory geography that is my body. Some folk understand fibroids to be made up of benign tissue representing and linked to intergenerational trauma. This is a theory I'm willing to accept without shame. Shame that I do not have time for in order to grow, create and breathe long and lasting breath. This is a choice that I've taken on this journey, especially now, inhabiting a heart that's healed, inhabiting all that depth and development, and I'm pregnant //

I'm pregnant with lion, despite the fibroids that took up the space in my belly. There is now a new life, temporarily encased by my womb. And though memories run deep and scars act as symbols to signify that it hasn't always been this way, the fact that the scars are there and that I can see them without hating anything about myself, in this body, in this life, makes me grateful and free. The scars show the endurance I have for being alive, the resilience of my ancestors and the fact that the fibroids are gone, offering space. I'm growing a new life; instead of fossilised fractals there is a new spine forming. As I grow, I'm accepting the gift of something that exists beyond my rational mind, in and out of my dreams like the swooping crane of luck in Asian mythology. This gift, like the serendipity in writing this book at the same time as my entire life is taking on a new chapter, like anything that grows and lives from the soil beneath me, in a world described as tired – this gift still hums life through the soles of my own dancing feet, connected to my right ankle, scarred from where I broke it hiking that day. I, we, are alive. Our bodies are known to communicate with the elements around us. Solidarity vibrates from within and rumbles outwards, chatting with water, ghosts, air and frequency and it cannot always be explained.

Over-questioning, too much screen time, transmitting quick promises . . . Distinguishing science from wisdom / feeling from hard facts / is more determined by my heart more active than it has ever been in my whole life. I am mostly in a state of thought and wonder for the many ways we can view and perceive our lived experience.

Meeting oneself in a world for us all.

It is now my baby's world that I have the honour of inhabiting and my faith in hope is enough. It's what I want to continue the most into the new role forming: mother. And yet I refuse to define an identity in the language of the colonial capitalist system, and it's only in the search for identity and love that I've been able to come to this way of being.

I searched everywhere for forgiveness and its meaning while walking through chaos.

Was it in my fusion DNA, I wondered? Where I hold so many shades of blue? I sat and bought myself a coffee and a cake the day I was notified that my DNA match results had come through. I sat upright and alert to learn the earthly clues to my traits, my weaknesses, my tenacity, perhaps even my fate . . . To discover I am, according to the website, 22 per cent Nigerian with other DNA matches in places expected and traced too . . . Ireland, Scotland especially. But also, gloriously not known before this moment, The Balkans, Sudan, Greece . . .

And there it was, my code, as broad as my emotions changing throughout a day under Scottish skies. Here I was, explained absurdly by percentages in a body I have learned to escape, an imagination expanded and quilted out of pain. Be it alcohol, sex, appeal, materiality, the nullification of each, all a search for love and for a self made up of so much. All a hunt for belonging and self-worth and suddenly my blood acted as enlightenment. For I am from everywhere and we all are and the love I have for living is in embracing our collective liberation. The results matched my method, my grounds, my career, the lessons, the emergence I feel. It has always been in an unwavering pursuit to unpick the connection I always feel to the living, the entanglement with my Sisterhood that has given me the gift of time travel and a chance to consolidate the searching fascination I have felt all my life. It is our honour to stand on the shoulders of:

Wang's ingenuity,
Pamela's mischief and intuition,
Una's conviction in the power of communication,
Audre's words and vitality that transcend her lifetime,
Jeanne's spellbinding resonance.
Grace Jones's eternal artistry,
Marsha's love, so true,
Mary W's heartfelt passion for travel,
Nanny's lifelong mission of justice,
Mary S's fortitude, recognised by her own self with courage,
Betty's honed talent,
Hatshepsut's mystery and beguilement,

Black experimental writing exists at the nexus of experience and open-ended endeavor without guarantees. It is a name, finally, for what I would now call a Black radical imagination, imagining new beginnings and beginning again, imagining possibilities beyond those

> already predicted by the present. This isn't the imagination that Black people have, but ways of surviving and producing the beauty necessary to sustain and nourish black lives, of reaching towards a future on terms other than those of the present.
>
> Anthony Reed, *Freedom Time: The Poetics and Politics of Black Experimental Writing*

There is something so odd about the silence of neglect – when your ideas come into fruition, but you're on the outside still of all that's actualised. Quietness should be soft and generative, but not when it's forced. I wonder if *The Immortal Sisterhood* is the matriarch I look for everywhere?

I've realised that the Earth is mother and that has made up for so much I have not had.

October 2024

In our rented flat and pretty tired.

I also shed a tear at the doctor's surgery the other week. Having stomped over in a spare hour of solo time having navigated the online portal in which you have to book in your appointment . . . I cried because I was tired, tired of too many portals on screens, too many passwords, access codes, AI-generated threats to peace of mind or the cultivation of common sense. I cried because I know I need support // old injuries, a neurodivergence (undiagnosed), the-coldness-of-winter-in-Scotland on a body that's not long ago had a baby for the first time. The doctor was great, the stigma around having to ask for some guidance in the overwhelm was smashed through for half an hour and I'm a tiny step closer to getting 'Access To Work', a governmental scheme which, albeit under threat, currently still exists to support the many of us who don't have 'typical' brains to actually do whatever it is we do for a living; support is something necessary, I've noticed, in many aspects of living and in my case especially as I'm getting older in combination with becoming a mother. I've spoken many times with my friends who are artists about how it's funny that art and the artist's process can be so romanticised even if it's been made through addled mental health / in among shadows and as catharsis for one's own trauma . . . It's more the potential healing in art that compels me the most. I crave being moved by more than just collective nihilism or pain, but by the miracle of its evaporation and the wonder in belonging if that pain is treated. Can the process and the product be one of shared pleasure or unselfconscious release? I feel this when getting my body to tune into the astral-skit opening to Grace Jones's 'My Jamaican Guy' when she makes a portal for the listener with the 'eh-ehhh' sound (go listen to it). I felt this when I went to see Judy Chicago's 'The Dinner Party' installation at the Brooklyn museum which is made up of a massive triangular shaped dinner table, complete with 39 intricate settings for different women in history (including Hatshepsut) and is full of symbology, shiny tiling and swirly writing, I feel this when I am in the sunshine by water and have some hours to read through a relic copy of *i-D* magazine from the 1980s.

What culture gets under your skin? Where do you feel your consciousness becomes more whole or enlightened? What art makes you glow and feel alive?

I hope you can remember to seek pleasure and don't let some of the notions (that hatred and anger sells and garners attention) and the corporatisation of creativity 'n' healing make you think you don't deserve it / can't access it . . . afford the money or time // see yourself in your own imagined flavour of your own cool, artful, blissful mecca in some of your free time. We can nurture ourselves with culture in so many ways for free. Please come with me in celebrating in ritual or in relaxation and rest in being seen, in being in community, in feeding ourselves in all the ways we can as humans – with shared music, food, movement, art and craft.

I hope, from my heart, that you have the encouragement and support to do so.

I imagined the freedom I needed to dream in the ancestral pedagogy of this process of mapping my Sisterhood. Certain words and the solitary regularity of writing them have become a sustainable practice and acupressure point of deep hope.

I invite you in, dear reader, to free up, and envelop yourself in the sparkle of this moment where grieving and rejoicing can exist at the same time, beyond an intellectual understanding, and grow our wild potential for great futures by both learning and unlearning in our present.

April 2025

Now that I'm 40, I'm learning the language of support. There's been a lot of shame seeping into asks for help over the years, a lot of fear about 'what it costs' to seek remedy, or for the judgement of the modality you choose when experimenting with therapy and medicine. I'm now seven months a mother, I've been forced to ask for help in a number of ways more recently: For example, I had to ask the funding body that rejected my application (five times) where I was going wrong and not let my body surge with over-apologising for my ideas when asking for nonsensical feedback to be broken down into something tangible.

The majority of the women in *The Immortal Sisterhood* documented something to carve out their legacy. For Mary Wollstonecraft, it was essays and letters; Mary Seacole, writing her own autobiography; Pamela Colman Smith, articles and drawings; Betty Davis, lyrics; Wang Zhenyi used the medium of poetry as one of her many forms of expression. While I studied this Hood, I read the poetry of Wang, Una, and Audre, poetry casting spells, words acting as weapons against confinement; I heard the tales and lessons in the music of Grace and Betty, read the published works of Mary S and Mary W, the letters to loved ones from Pamela; I started to hear similarity in their rallying calls. I feel humble at the reclamation of the history these womxn told very much in their own work.

December 2025
In the library in Edinburgh

Dear Sisters

Quick one.

Oh goodness. I'm pregnant, AGAIN. So much more quickly after lion-Rita than I would have planned. The baby will be born before the book is officially published. Serves me right, for all the abundance I ask for when I light candles. The internet says three years is the perfect gap between babies, this'll be less than that. It feels like a pure love boon. But my god, how will I be able to hold it all down? Where do we go from here? This is the first year of my life that more than one friend has told me that it's impossible to be happy in this world, with how it is. How do I build a world for my family that stands with beauty, truth, but also serenity, and protection with all that I've had my eyes and heart cracked open during this writing process?

New little Lion: I'm unsure how I'll explain the world to you. Its darkness runs heavy, but it's in newness that I've always found so much light, and in your life, I hope we can protect your hope. We'll build it together with your sister and dad and I commit to never needing anything from you but to be your protector, as you orientate and breathe in a world anew.

I'm excited to try to create great and wonderful times.

Gemma
Xx

NOTES

Author's Note

1 A 'slashie' was a term for a multi-hyphenate soul seeker at the time I was living in East London in the 2000s. I felt like I was a walking heartbeat of all that was happenin' back then and was young enough to not feel the cold on my bare legs: if I felt my outfit was fantastic then the adrenaline would keep me warm. It was 2007, before the 'Credit Crunch', and many of us had studied some kinda art and been led to fashion in the hope it would be possible for us to be models / writers / dreamers / fashionistas / performers / pop stars / presenters / artists / butterflies. Slashin' in fashion. Slayin' & sashayin' & still be able to afford to live.

1. Wang Zhenyi

1 A radio series about musical collaboration that I did two seasons of. I loved working on it. Documenting and recording on the move, and capturing the feel of a place through the textures of sound and conversation, is up there with some of my most important memories. I'll play the series to my daughter one day. It'll allow us to sonically transport ourselves to Colombia, Ghana, Lebanon, Guyana, Morocco and Ethiopia.

2 'Trailblazers - The Age of Girls: Wany Zheny' by Tia Shah, The Girl Museum, Inc. 24 May 2018.

3 Peterson, Barbara Bennett (2000). *Notable Women of China: Shang Dynasty to the Early Twentieth Century*. New York: M. E. Sharp. pp. 341–345.

4 One of Wang's other famous papers was 'Explanation of The Starry, Starry Sky'. She's now become one of the very stars. In 1994 the International Astronomical Union's Working Group for Planetary System Nomenclature named a crater on Venus after her.

5 There are similar stories of creatures eating the sun and/or moon in so many other cultures. In Norse mythology it's two wolves called Sköll and Hati who chase the sun and moon. In Hinduism it's the celestial beings Rahu and Ketu. Interestingly, eclipses can appear linked to uprisings. In February 1831, in the Southern state of Virginia in the United States, an educated preacher and enslaved man called Nat Turner saw a solar eclipse as a sign that it was time to begin a revolt against enslavement. He described the vision he had during an eclipse as a Black man's hands over the sun. In West Africa, the Batammaliba people of Northern Togo and Benin have a legend about the world's first women, Puka Puka and Kuiyecoke, who were tasked with keeping peace between villages. To show people they really meant business, Puka Puka and Kuiyecoke used their powers to darken the skies by directing the moon and sun into an eclipse. In their collective need to see in the dark, villages created peace with one another so they could all find their way, which eventually led to them working together on the land. These people may have been guided by these legends – by Puka Puka and Kuiyecoke coming together to shake up the sky – towards centuries of social and agricultural progress.

2. Pamela Colman Smith

1 The rest of the quotation reads: 'Banish fear, brace your courage, place your ideal high up with the sun, away from the dirt and

squalor and ugliness around you and let that power that makes 'the roar of the high-power presses' enter into your work – energy – courage – life – love. Use your wits, use your eyes. Perhaps you use your physical eyes too much and only see the mask. Find eyes within, look for the door into the unknown country.'

2 Yemoja / Yemaya / Yemanja / Lemanja is the mother of all Orishas in Yoruba belief and her element is the sea (a deity / goddess in West African and Afro-Brazilian traditions). Her symbols include the cowrie shell and she is as powerful as oceans. If angered, she can unleash tsunamis.

3 Coding as we know it today is still a kind of magic and is known mostly for its use in visual creation and sharing knowledge on the internet. But humans have always been forming code: the ancient Egyptians communicated through hieroglyphs and vast symbolic systems, as did the Celts, Aztecs, Greeks, Romans, Minoans, and Persians. How are tools such as sigils (inscribed or painted symbols considered to have magical power), shape, native language, astrocartography (a form of astrology that creates a world map signifying where the planets were positioned at the time of someone's birth), and wisdom-filled myth and fable so hidden from curious global feminists?

4 Forty thousand to sixty thousand women were murdered in the witch hunts in Europe. A particular concentration of trials occurred in and around Edinburgh in the 1590s, often resulting in cruel public torture within the grounds of the very castle I walk past several times a week. These were often women with specialist knowledge of herbs, roots, and nature – who acted as doctors or midwives in their communities – or fortune-tellers who were specifically targeted.

5 According to Greek mythology, Melia (also Meilae or Melie) are the nymphs or goddesses of the ash tree. The ash tree, in Celtic folklore, is revered for its divine ability to protect and heal. Some

call it the Tree of Life. Traditionally, when a child is born, its sap is collected by midwives, and its bark is used to make wooden staffs to connect with higher realms.

3. Una Marson

1 Brent Hayes Edwards, *The Practice of Diaspora: Literature, Translation, and the Rise of Black Internationalism* (Cambridge MA: Harvard University Press, 2003)

4. Audre Lorde

1 Audre Lorde, *Uses of the Erotic: The Erotic as Power*, in *Sexualities and Communication in Everyday Life: A Reader* (India: SAGE Publications, 2007), 89.

2 Scott Edwards, 'Dancing and the Brain', Harvard Medical School, 2015, https://hms.harvard.edu/news-events/publications-archive/brain/dancing-brain; Ian Tucker, 'Peter Lovatt: "Dancing Can Change the Way You Think"', *The Guardian*, 31 July 2011.

3 Xicanisma is the most recent intervention in the decolonial practice, originally known as Chicana, of womxn with Mexican heritage.

5. Jeanne Duval

1 The name given to the earth by the Lenape people who originally inhabited the island of Manhattan (which took its name from the Lenape word 'manahahtaan') and its surrounding areas.

7. Marsha P. Johnson

1 Quoted in Sewell Chan, 'Marsha P. Johnson: A Transgender Pioneer and Activist Who Was a Fixture of Greenwich Village

Street Life,' *The New York Times*, March 8, 2018, https://www.nytimes.com/interactive/2018/obituaries/overlooked-marsha-p-johnson.html

2 The Onyx is a jet-black gemstone associated with strength, protection and courage.

3 https://www.biography.com/activists/marsha-p-johnson

8. Mary Wollstonecraft

1 In astrology, Taurus is represented by the Bull figure and is known for persistent and tenacious characteristics.

2 A strawberry moon is a rare lunar occurrence that not only lights up the sky like a sweet, celestial feast of ripe summer glowing pinks and indigo romance, but is also associated with good harvest and named by the tribes of Native America for its association with true abundance, and emotional renewal. This is Robin Wall Kimmerer a mother, scientist, decorated professor, and enrolled member of the Citizen Potawatomi Nation, in her book *Braiding Sweetgrass*: 'Even now, after more than fifty Strawberry Moons, finding a patch of wild strawberries still touches me with a sensation of surprise, a feeling of unworthiness and gratitude for the generosity and kindness that comes with an unexpected gift all wrapped in red and green'.

3. 'Maternal mortality rates in the Black community', The Lords Library. 12 December 2023. https://lordslibrary.parliament.uk/maternal-mortality-rates-in-the-black-community/

9. Nanny of the Maroons

1 Maroons were among the most resilient and powerful people in the Caribbean – the ones who during the time of slavery ran away, often into nature. Spanish Town in Jamaica is where the Spanish

originally tried to take the island, having slaughtered most of the indigenous people (the Arawak) who lived there.

2 There's a Rastafarian phrase that I love and that says so much: 'I for I'. As an incantation, it has so many meanings: I as in you and I; as in us as much part of nature as nature is part of us.

3 Eartha Kitt wasn't born in Jamaica, but like many enslaved Jamaican she was born on a plantation, in a small town in South Carolina, USA. Her mum was of African and Cherokee descent; her father was said to be a white man with Dutch or German heritage. He may have been the plantation owner's son and – if so – it's possible (if not likely) that Eartha was born from rape. Even her name appears to link to the struggle for land that Nanny exemplified. 'Eartha' may have come from the Anglo Saxon word 'ertha' meaning soil, or the Dutch 'aerde', or the Old German 'erda'. It all leads back to the same thing: women, Black women, being from the earth, knowing the earth, knowing its importance, yearning to return to it, free from assimilation.

10. Mary Seacole

1 I can't help thinking about the sounds of bells and their association with heaven. The earliest known advent of bells dates to around 3500 BCE in China, where bronze bell casts have been found – some used to make bells weighing hundreds of pounds. Since then, bells have been associated with marking holy times or points in the day. In the Middle Ages superstition held that bells would ring themselves to warn of danger.

2. Quoted in Bedour Alagraa, 'What Will Be the Cure?: A Conversation with Sylvia Wynter', *Offshoot Magazine*, 7 January 2021, https://offshootjournal.org/what-will-be-the-cure-a-conversation-with-sylvia-wynter/

11. Betty Davis

1 Quoted in Fiona Shepherd, 'Obituary: Betty Davis, Flamboyant Funk Singer Famed for Raucous Performances,' *The Scotsman*, 25 February 2022, https://www.scotsman.com/news/people/obituary-betty-davis-flamboyant-funk-singer-famed-for-raucous-performances-3584543

12. Pharaoh Hatshepsut

1 In Kemetic tradition, the lotus mimics the sun with its daily cycle of death and rebirth / rising and setting / opening and closing. Depictions of the dead in tomb murals show them smelling flowers to infuse their souls with the power of Ra (the Sun god). The ancients were not shy about their love for the striking blue lotus flower growing along the Nile. Maybe we could learn from them by filling our life with flowers?

2 Jason Pohl, 'Investigating the Psychedelic Blue Lotus of Egypt, Where Ancient Magic Meets Modern Science,' *UC Berkeley News*, March 11, 2025, https: //news.berkeley.edu/2025/03/11/ investigating-the-psychedelic-blue-lotus-of-egypt-where-ancient-magic-meets-modern-science /

Afterword

1 Prende is the folkloric Albanian deity of the sky. It's said that she wears rainbows for a belt that connects her to a chariot led by swallows that pull her through the sky.

BIBLIOGRAPHY

Bergdorf, Munroe. *Transitional: In One Way or Another, We All Transition*. London: Bloomsbury, 2023.

Brown, Adrienne Maree. *Pleasure Activism: The Politics of Feeling Good*. Chico, CA: AK Press, 2019.

Chicago, Judy. *Through the Flower: My Struggle as a Woman Artist*. New York: Doubleday, 1975.

Grajkowski, Wojciech & Socha, Piotr. *The Book of Bees*. London: Thames & Hudson, 2021.

Hartman, Saidiya. *Wayward Lives, Beautiful Experiments: Intimate Histories of Riotous Black Girls, Troublesome Women, and Queer Radicals*. London: Serpent's Tail, 2019.

Hersey, Tricia. *Tricia Hersey – Rest is Resistance: A Manifesto*. New York: Little, Brown, 2022.

Kinouani, Guilaine. *Living While Black: The Essential Guide to Overcoming Racial Trauma*. London: Bloomsbury, 2021.

Lorde, Audre. *A Land From Where Other People Live*. Detroit: Broadside Lotus Press, 1973.

Lorde, Audre. *Burst of Light*. Ithaca, NY: Firebrand Books, 1988.

Lorde, Audre. *The Cancer Journals*. San Francisco: Spinsters Ink, 1980.

Lorde, Audre. *The Black Unicorn*. New York: W.W. Norton, 1978.

Lorde, Audre. *Zami: A New Spelling of My Name: A Biomythography*. Watertown, MA: Persephone Press, 1982.

Marson, Una. *The Moth and The Star*. Kingston: The Gleaner Co., 1937.

Ravn, Olga. *My Work*. London: Lolli Editions, 2023.

Reed, Anthony. *Freedom Time: The Poetics and Politics of Black Experimental Writing*. Baltimore: Johns Hopkins University Press, 2014.

Rowlatt, Bee. *In Search of Mary: The Mother of All Journeys*. London: Alma Books, 2015.

Seacole, Mary. *Wonderful Adventures of Mrs Seacole in Many Lands*. London: James Blackwood, 1857.

Shange, Ntozake. *For Colored Girls Who Have Considered Suicide / When the Rainbow Is Enuf*. New York: Macmillan, 1977.

Solnit, Rebecca. *Hope in the Dark: The Untold Story of People Power*. Edinburgh: Canongate, 2004.

Stryker, Susan. *Transgender History: The Roots of Today's Revolution*. New York: Seal Press, 2017.

Tourmaline. *Marsha: The Joy and Defiance of Marsha P. Johnson*. New York: Penguin, 2025.

Tyldesley, Joyce. *Hatshepsut: The Female Pharaoh*. London: Penguin, 1998.

Walker, Christopher. *Nanny of the Maroons*. Independently published, 2025.

ACKNOWLEDGEMENTS

With thanks to my beautiful, adventurous family
Cameron, Rita and the new sun in my tum.

Working fellowship in The Immortal Sisterhood LIVE ensemble
Roxanne, Simone (lil sib), Amelia, Mele

The ardent cheerleaders, Col & Susan, Beth, Dawn, Debz, Gup 'n Gup . . .

collaborators Rebecca, Alice, Wezi, Gen

and all the cracking chosen fam and friends . . .

of whom, without I'm not sure what I'd do . . .

Thank you to my sis Laura you have taught me real Sisterhood.

Thank you Hannah and Becky for nurturing the seeds of writing.

Thank you Mother and every mother for all the lessons.

Thank you Dad for teaching me unconditionality.

AND EVERYbody else . . . well.

Please forgive me, I'm sorry if it ain't your cup of tea. I love you